Poison to
PURPOSE

To.

Dejuai

From

Dwaun

LOVE

Always

Poison to Purpose: A Gospel Legend's Journey

ISBN 978-1-7321325-5-9

Copyright (c) 2019 by Duranice Pace

Published by:

Noahs Ark Publishing Service
8549 Wilshire Blvd., Suite 1442
Beverly Hills, CA 90211
www.noahsarkpublishing.com

Edited by Elyse Wietstock
Graphic Design by Christopher C. White and James Sparkman

Poison to PURPOSE

A GOSPEL LEGEND'S JOURNEY

DURANICE PACE

Noahs Ark Publishing Service
Beverly Hills, California

I dedicate this book to my one and only son, DeMarcus.

*You never stopped loving and believing in
me. Through all of my painful mental and
physical challenges, you never left my side and
dutifully prayed for me without ceasing.*

*You saw me at my worst and never made me feel
awkward or ugly. You fed and bathed me when I
didn't have the strength to lift my own hands.*

*For eight years, you unselfishly and lovingly served me.
I am standing today because of God's glorious grace
and you, my beautiful son. Thank you, DeMarcus.
I love you beyond what words can express.*

Contents

Introduction

The word poison conjures up an image in my mind that is found on old dark bottles containing highly toxic and flammable mixtures like arsenic, cyanide and other strong chemicals. Substances like this are generally used to exterminate rodents in apartment buildings and houses or to clean hardened gunk off of equipment and floors found in industrial facilities. The containers were placed on the highest shelf in a broom closet or underneath the bathroom or kitchen sink to keep children unaware of its existence. An artful skull and crossbones usually accompanied the word, which really made one a bit timid to even touch the container without gloves. After using these solutions, hands should be washed to keep any residue from getting on the skin or in the eyes. If swallowed, death could be imminent, unless a hospital emergency team was able to flush it out of the human system.

The dictionary definition refers to poison as any substance that causes injury, illness, or death of a living organism, or the act of giving it to someone. Have you ever watched a frightening murder mystery or soap opera drama and followed the villain as he or she slipped a dose of poison into someone's drink or food? The sole purpose of doing so was to kill the person and permanently erase their existence or ability to influence, create, or sustain life.

The word poison can be a metaphorical reference. Have you ever been in the presence of someone whose attitude poisoned your environment? Their endless chatter could potentially spoil a good mood and taint the vibes of a positive event. Twitter, Instagram, and Facebook have become storage bins for poisonous trolls' spewing, and certain hierarchy who desire to turn the opinions of their readers and viewers to their narcissistic philosophies.

In whatever form it appears, it is dangerous. Poison was created to disable and deconstruct. Its prime intent is to remove, and its strength can destroy the best of us if we are faint of heart.

In this book, I speak from both positions. Literal and metaphorical, as I have been affected by both, starting in my mother's womb.

Some of you are already sensing the direction I am going with this. Your soul is picking up my tone without hearing anything about my life's journey. Others could be oblivious or even disconnected from the essence in the words I write. Because the poison you've consumed, whether voluntarily or by force, have numbed your feelings which are likely buried deep within your subconscious, to keep you from losing your natural mind. I get it! I've been there!

Listen, in this life hardship and struggle are guaranteed to visit. Hardship and Struggle show up in pairs right to your doorstep, sometimes by surprise and when you least expect it. Not only do they show up at your doorstep, they open the door without your permission, don't wipe their feet on the doormat, and bring their dirt from outside into your home. With entitlement, they take a seat on your best furniture and expect to be served. If we are honest, we have waited on them hand and foot by giving in to their requests. If Hardship says, "Lay down!" in the midst of oppression, we obey it. If Struggle yells out, "Give up," we throw in the towel at its command. Young or old, many can attest to the fact that what I am saying is pure truth!

This book is mainly written to you who have been oppressed and poisoned in your minds. To those whose thinking is distorted because the layers of venom spewed upon you over time have hardened. To you who are losing your faith in God, the Creator of all things; the Omnipotent, Omnipresent One who knows and sees all, every second of every hour, 7 days a week, 365 days a year and throughout eternity! The One whose ways are not our ways, nor his thoughts our thoughts, but He is working everything, and I repeat, *everything*, out for our total good if we yield Him clearance to do so. This book is for you!

I know what it's like to be loved and admired and then shoved off the pedestal others placed me on.

I understand what it feels like to be told, "You will never succeed in a great way because you are not smart like the others."

I have smelled the stench of death as it crossed right in front of me, grabbed me by my neck to try and steal the breath from my lungs.

Have you ever been given a time limit of three years left on your life? I have, but as you can see, I am still here on planet Earth and thriving 11 years after that prognosis.

You can't tell me miracles aren't real and that God doesn't exist because he showed up for me and He will do the same for you.

Find yourself a comfortable chair and turn off any unnecessary outside noise. I pray that my testimony will enlighten, invigorate, and move you to pursue God and all that He has for you.

"For I know the plans I have for you," declares the LORD, "plans to prosper you and not to harm you, plans to give you hope and a future."

Jeremiah 29:11.

Chapter 1

I'm Gonna Sing on Broadway

Many of us have experienced having that one teacher whose motivation changed the course and trajectory of our lives. Mrs. Wilder was the one for me. She was a phenomenal teacher who taught chorus. I loved singing in the school chorus. When teaching music workshops all over the country I encourage attendees to join their school chorus. Chorus teachers are thoroughly equipped. They are college educated, know vocals, can teach you how to strengthen your voice, train your ear, and teach music theory. While it's good that many singers have voices that can almost lift the roofs off of buildings, it is vital that we take our God-given gifts and continually strengthen them. Singing in the school chorus fine-tuned my voice.

I started chorus in middle school and participated all the way through high school until graduation. There were two schools in my small town, Harper Elementary and Joyce High School. This was great because the teachers and principals really got to know their students and families well. There were teacher and parent nights that took place once a month. If you got into the music or theatrical departments you could easily make friends. We knew everybody back in our childhood days and I loved that. Unlike current times, schools were very family oriented. Nowadays, many kids seem to be on their own. Young people seem to keep to themselves and don't take time to form healthy playground relationships. My desire is that school administrations throughout the country would take a closer look at this important developmental foundation.

All of my sisters and my brother sang in the chorus. There were eleven of us. Murphy was the first of my siblings to join and he encouraged each one of us to do the same. My brother led his life like that. Singing in the chorus got your name out all over the school, making you quite popular. Though six of us studied in different classrooms, chorus brought us together. We were very excited to see each other at practice and always greeted each other enthusiastically as if we hadn't seen each other in weeks! This surprised and humored our fellow students! I guess they were thinking, "didn't they see each other before they came to school and won't they see each other when they get home?" I get their point, but hey, we not only loved each other, but liked each other and never tired of being together. People would see us and say things like, "Oh there goes one of those singers! She's from the Pace family and there's a lot of them! They're all in the chorus and they can sing!"

Mrs. Wilder not only taught us different songs, but we also learned how to read music and expertly discern notes. Yearly competitions between schools was a highlight and we won every year.

Our town's elementary school didn't have a chorus so my one and only, very outgoing brother, started a youth program and choir at our church, Valley View Church of God in Christ. Our Pastor, Superintendent John Cooper knew Murphy would become a pastor one day so allowing him to grow in leadership was a no-brainer. Murphy tried new things and had many excellent ideas that were implemented within the department. His skills and abilities were undeniable and before long he was appointed Youth Pastor.

We were very proud of our brother and excited to help him out any way we could. As a result, we all grew within the music ministry.

Around this time our family singing group was formed. First Lady Brinson lived near us in Pool Creek, our neighborhood community, and came to visit our mother one day. She told her, "Mother Pace, have you noticed that your children have beautiful voices?" Our mother explained that everyone had been so busy doing other things for the church and hadn't paid much attention. Sister Brinson suggested to our mother that she allow us to start singing as the Pace Family. She said, "If you do this, I will help you! We have a program once a month on Sundays at 3:00 p.m. and I want you all to come and sing. If you can get them there, I will get people and other groups to come and I will organize it for you. The Lord told me to tell you that your children have beautiful voices. Pray about letting them start as a family group." Sister Brinson already had success orchestrating singing groups. She had nine boys and started them singing, playing guitar, bass, and drums. She was head of the group and would lead out singing. They called themselves Mom Brinson and the Brinson Brothers.

Sis. Brinson started our group, The Pace Family, with nine girls and one boy. She was a woman of her word and consistent. Her church was only about fifteen to twenty minutes from ours. The programs she coordinated there were very popular. As we started singing at her events more often, word got around and people began asking my mother to let us sing at their programs. Mrs. Brinson was very smart and predicted this would happen! The Pace Family became well known in the city of Atlanta. We started singing all over the city. We traveled from Atlanta to its outskirts, and after a period of time we were singing throughout the entire state of Georgia. Traveling around the state and knowing people wanted us and enjoyed hearing us sing was all very exciting. Daddy made sure our car ran well and Mother had enough gas to get us to our destinations. We loved riding in our yellow and brown station wagon because it had seats in the very back that faced the traffic. Four of us could easily fit back there and to be fair, we all had to switch out. We had so much fun!

Our trips were well planned. People would call us way ahead of time to secure dates. If traveling a great distance, we would wake up at 6:00 a.m. on Saturday mornings to make sure we arrived on time. Daddy paid for gas and the hotel, and Mother made snacks that fit into two picnic baskets. She made bologna sandwiches, fried chicken and Kool-Aid. I'll never forget it.

That's how we got started. I have to give Sister Brinson her props. If she hadn't spoken to my mother that one fateful day, we may not have taken the leap. She broadened our education in music, and we thank God for her.

We stayed a family group until everybody graduated high school. Invitations to participate in events out of state were coming to us more frequently, but Daddy said we had to graduate first before traveling outside of Georgia. Our dad believed education was more important so once we finished high school, Daddy felt we were ready.

～ The Anointed Pace Sisters ～

My brother went on to attend college and that made us feel so sad. It felt like he was leaving for good, but Dad reassured us that we'd be alright. The Lord knew what He was doing. The name of our group changed from the Pace Family to the Anointed Pace Sisters!

There was a man named Elder Carol Lester Morell who was known for playing the tambourine and dancing. He was the one who told our mother to name us the Anointed Pace Sisters. We had a lot of help that came from Church of God in Christ folks. There were a lot of extended family members who helped us make the climb to working as professionals. Also, Dr. Romini Howard who oversaw the COGIC Sunshine Band for years gave us our first anniversary service and bought us our first uniforms. They were purple! Beautiful purple long dresses!

The first anniversary was breathtaking. Over ten choirs, several groups, quartets, and solo artists came to support and celebrate with us. Our way was paid for and three thousand dollars was raised, which at that time was a lot of money to us. That money was placed in an account and was only to be used for traveling expenses to our various engagements. That tremendous blessing took the financial burden off of Daddy.

Every engagement taught us more about the business side of the music industry. Some would give us sixty dollars here and a hundred dollars there. When we started getting three hundred dollars, we thought we were rich! Daddy counted it all out at the dinner table. We paid our tithes and whatever else we needed was paid for from what we made at the services. We were very excited, and Daddy was our number one fan!

Singing for the Lord is beautifully overwhelming and sometimes met with tears. Daddy taught us to not stop singing when we felt the Holy Spirit moving. He said, "Keep on ministering!" He also taught us stage presence.

My Dad was a professional singer with a group called the Spiritual Starlights. They were gospel stars at the time and sharp with their black processed hair and beautiful white teeth. They rehearsed every Wednesday in our living room, and all of them smoked cigars. Our father wasn't saved at the time but sang in this quartet for eighteen to twenty years. He was very professional and so was my mother. Mother sang a lot of the sermonic solos before pastors would speak, but Daddy was the true professional. The Spiritual Starlights had multiple suits and shoes alike. They owned their sound systems and instruments. So Dad knew what he was talking about when instructing us on stage presence. He taught us to not just stand there looking at the floor while we sang, but to come down into the audience, shake folks' hands, and look people in the eyes.

There was a time when he took us all into downtown Atlanta to watch him sing with his group. We were so proud and would exclaim to each other, "That's my daddy, that's my daddy!" He would come walking down the stage by himself and folks would start throwing money at him! He told me to pick the money up. Wads of it was everywhere. I'd take the money to Mother, and she'd put it in her purse. We were so proud of him as he smiled at us from the stage with those pretty white teeth and processed hair. We wanted to be just like him!

In 1985, Shaun was the one that Savoy Records first signed as a solo artist. We initially thought she was being torn away from the family. We cried about it for a while, but also learned invaluable lessons from the experience. Shaun began to record in the studio by herself. She came back and shared with us the dos and don'ts, how to carry yourself in a hotel, contracts and how to write them, etc. Shaun saw something in me and told me I was going to be a solo artist one day too. She encouraged me and soothed my feelings by teaching me how companies can't always afford to sign a lot of artists, so they picked one and she was just the first one. The first year was tough but the second year was better. Shaun would go on the road, make money and bring it back home to help the family. She was blessed with an awesome career.

Gene Martin, a member of the A.A. Allen Evangelistic Party, travelled the road often. He became a very close and wonderful friend of our family. We called him Uncle Gene. Uncle Gene asked our mother if we could tour with him for three months over the summer. He said he would make sure we had food, a place to stay, be given an honorarium, and could talk to our parents every day. Our parents gave him the green light and we were off! He took us to California, where we first visited Ernestine Cleveland Reems' church in Oakland. From there we went to Los Angeles, and last to San Diego.

Gene gave all of us parts. He'd say, "Here Shaun, you lead this song, Phyllis you lead this song." The audience responded to each of us differently. I started singing more solos.

Uncle Gene introduced us to a lot of people that were in plays, like the very popular, *Your Arms Too Short to Box with God.* We got to meet people one-on-one through him and they gave him tickets for us to come and see plays. We got to meet Walter and Edwin Hawkins backstage. Because of Uncle Gene, we met the great Timothy Wright and Thomas Whitfield before he died. Thomas would take us out to dine with him when he came through Atlanta. Rance Allen sat in my momma's living room and ate her fried chicken and collard greens. DJ Rogers also came to our house and sang at our church. Uncle Gene introduced us to people we would have never met. They were all excellent songwriters and their music sold into the millions of dollars. The Anointed Pace Sisters were honored to sing their songs. It took our breath away.

We stayed committed to our COGIC state and national choirs and never got too high and mighty. Dr. Clark, the highly esteemed International COGIC Music Minister for many years, gave me parts in the state and national choirs.

It's no wonder I developed dreams to one day perform… Watching my dad sing under the spotlight on stage was electrifying and mesmerizing, to say the least.

When we Pace children were very young we had entertainment icons we loved to watch on television and movie theater screens. We loved Shirley Temple, Doris Day and Julie Andrews, and musicals like *Chitty Chitty Bang Bang, Mary Poppins*, and *FAME!*

One of our most favorite television shows was *FAME!* Every day for five years straight we watched Debbie Allen and all of the talented youth perform and we were mesmerized! It was a beautiful musical show that our parents allowed us to watch on television once our chores around the house were done. Our eyes would be glued to the television screen. We watched every move, learned every song and could visualize ourselves doing the same thing.

I am enamored with the Broadway stages of New York City. When I was eight years old, I knew I had to make it to the Big Apple. I had to make my mark in the city that never sleeps. The deep desire to move there and perform in a Broadway musical with other phenomenal singers and actors continues to burn deep within my heart. I believe I was born to do it and that God planted that special ambition deep in the soil of my soul. That's why I cannot let it go! I'm hungry for it and believe God has something waiting for me there. I know that I'm supposed to stand right smack dab in the middle of one of those magnificent stages and sing my heart out! But it can't just be about performing. Performing is a great perk and very cool, but with God, there is always more waiting behind the divine curtain. Timing is everything with God… you know what I mean?

Pastor Carter Conlon is the pastor of Time Square Church. He saw me being interviewed by Mr. Steve Harvey on the Steve Harvey Show in Los Angeles, CA. While he was watching, he said the Lord told him to bring me to his church and introduce me to Broadway. Pastor Conlon purchased *Lion King* tickets for me, my sister Lydia and my manager, Cornelius. Boy when I tell you I cried like a baby, believe you me, I cried like a big ol' baby! I was so happy, thankful, grateful, excited and ecstatic all at the same time! If you have never been to New York, trust me when I tell you, it is fascinating! Creativity owns the sidewalks there and it shoots through you once you set foot on the pavement. The city is alive, and it made me feel more alive! Take my word for it and go see for yourselves. For those of you who have already visited, the next time you see me in person, just slide me a high five or give me a fist pump, look me in the eye and say, "You ain't never lied sis!"

I strolled down Broadway and stepped inside the theater to see *The Lion King*. After the cast took their final bow, I was brought backstage and introduced to them and so many other wonderful people who brought the play to life. The agent looked at me and said, "We heard about you through Steve Harvey and learned that one of your dreams is to sing on Broadway." Then she moved in closer and looked at me harder and said, "...and we are going to make it happen. We're just trying to figure out which show. You can do several!" Then she said to one of her colleagues, "Let her do *Mahalia Sings!*" This woman, who was like an angel to me, called out about three shows and said, "You can bank on that!" Then she grabbed me, gave me a great big warm hug and asked if I would sing the song, "I Will Always Be" for them. Do you think I hesitated? My oh my, I had never been so honored. The song burst from my spirit and I baptized them in that song in the rear of that Broadway

Theater stage! After I sang she said, "Duranice, if you don't already know, not only are you and your sisters legends, *YOU* are a legend. The Lord is going to take you to places you would never believe you would go. I will teach you as well. We are saved." Everyone around her started nodding their heads up and down in affirmation. They said they all wanted to meet the legend that wrote the song, "I Will Always Be." By now you know that I'm a crier and once again, I did cry. I am not ashamed of my tears. She said they were so happy that I came and even happier that I came backstage. I remain humbled that they all wanted to meet me.

The road to finally reaching our goals and dreams is sometimes long and winding but the lessons, skills, and wisdom we learn along the way are invaluable. Starting with my family singing at the neighborhood church services, then traveling within and outside of the city of Atlanta and across the U.S. took many years to achieve.

At this point, you might be questioning the title of this book. I can hear your thoughts reader and if I were in your position, I might be saying some of the same things. "This sounds like such a nice story. It is not dark at all. You had support from your parents, siblings, and teachers. You were given great favor from people in the church who believed in your talent, potential and ultimate success. These people helped you become a professional. You got to travel and do what you love to do, all over your city, state, and eventually the country and got paid to do it. You got to do things most people only dream of doing and it seems like it was just placed in your hands on a bed of roses. Where is the poison, Duranice?"

I am no different than you. The enemy who is also your enemy set out to disrupt everything you have read about thus far. Before I was born, he tried to abort my life when my mother was pregnant with me.

She suffered a big fall which caused me to be born two months premature. As a child, I suffered with terrible feelings of low self-esteem. I was constantly reminded that I was born early and would never develop to my full mental capacity. I have suffered physical ailments that literally tried to destroy my voice so that I would never speak or sing again.

I have gone through hell and back while walking out my God-given purpose. But I was never alone in the process and thank the Lord, you don't have to be either!

❦

Chapter 2

It Happened So Quickly

My grandmother on my mother's side was just awesome! Her name was Inell Gambel Couch. She had her own restaurant, but back then it was called a Juke Joint. It had cement floors, tables, and chairs and ashtrays at each table. I used to empty those ashtrays for her. Murphy being the oldest, then me, and Phyllis who is right under me, would help sweep the floors and keep the place clean. Grandmother was a short order cook and sold chicken, hamburgers and hot dogs. She also made some of the best soul food dinners with chitlins, collard greens, and cornbread. We were crazy about her!

After many years, she unfortunately suffered a stroke and couldn't do a lot of things she used to do. She owned two homes at that time. They were shotgun houses. You could look up and see straight through the house. Her house was located in the back by the Coca-Cola machine. She owned all of that. Her son, the baby boy, lived in the front. Sometimes I would go and help her. One day she asked my mother if I could stay with her for a full day to help out and my mother said yes. My grandmother was so appreciative. I stayed with her and helped her clean, dust, and get things in order. She was very neat, and it bothered her that she couldn't keep her home as tidy as she could prior to having the stroke. One time she was fixing some hot water cornbread and some of her delicious soup. She asked me to take a plate to my uncle. To get to his place you had to walk up these little stairs to a screen door. His wood door was open, so I said, "Uncle Petey, Granny told me to bring you your food."

Well, it all happened so quickly and my God, it was scary! I did not know my uncle could move so fast because he was an alcoholic. Before I could get all the words out of my mouth, he opened that screen door and the food went flying as he lifted me up in the air and turned toward his bed. All I know is that I was on the bed and he had stripped my clothes off of me. I had a skirt and top on. He stripped my skirt and undergarments off and had gotten on me. I was only twelve years old. I was very confused and hurting because the pain from all of it was so bad. I thought that I might even be having a nightmare because it was so horrible! I had never felt that kind of pain before. My grandmother sensed something was wrong. She could only use her right arm. She couldn't do a lot with it but there was a little strength left. Before I knew it my grandmother had a broomstick and she was up those stairs and was hitting him with it until the bottom part of that broom came off. She was yelling at him saying, "Get off her, get off her! What's wrong with you! Have you lost your mind?! Get off her!" All I could do was scream and cry out for my mom, "Mommy! I want my mommy!" I cried and I cried. He ran down the steps and out of the house and disappeared for about two days. He got scared knowing my daddy had been in the military. My uncle had also been in the military. My grandmother grabbed me. I was bleeding so bad. He tore my hymen and stole my virginity. I had to go to the hospital, have surgery, and take medication. I spotted for three months and that was another layer of fear placed on me. Dr. McCree gave my mother these tiny red pills that helped me heal. It was touch and go for a minute. If the blood thickened and continued to flow then I would have had a serious problem, but as long as the blood thinned out and minor spotting occurred I was safe. Eventually, I healed. From that time on I was scared to death of my uncle until he died.

My brother came up to me and grabbed me while I was healing, and he said "Niecy, I'm so sorry about what he did to you because he did it to me when I went to help Grandmama one day too. I went to the store and had to go through the woods. Remember that part in the woods where we used to hold hands real tight when we had to go to the store? Well, I ran through there all by myself and I thought I would be all right, but he had a limb and tripped me up." He was smart, very smart. Going to the store wasn't a problem but coming back is when he tripped my brother. Grandmama again knew that something was wrong. She took off walking, going through those woods to the store and there she found him. My uncle had a real bad spirit when it came to molesting children. I found out later that what he had done to me and my brother he had also done to about 6 of my cousins, we just didn't know it at the time.

That's why my mother had to fast. She could do a 21-day fast like it was nothing. A 3-day fast was nothing for her. She would do those 21-day fasts and more, drinking liquids only. She would pray and anoint us every day. Me being the oldest made her even more protective of the other ones. None of my other siblings ever went to or stayed at their house again.

One would think that you could trust your fellow church parishioners, but that is unfortunately not always the case.

Two girls that my mom picked from the church molested me, my brother Murphy and my sister Phyllis. These girls were bullies and used a belt to make my brother lay on us and do things. God told my mother to come home early from work one day and led her to park next door at

Miss Bell's house. My mom walked from Ms. Bell's to our yard and the Lord again led her to go to the second window. She went to the second window and it happened to be up and open and the babysitters didn't realize it. My mother stood there for the longest time and heard everything. She called out their names. One was the missionary's daughter and the other belonged to the pastor. They jumped up and gasped when they heard their names being called. One of them said, "Who said that?" and my mother answered, "I did, I'm out here." and they said, "Mother Pace?" She said, "Yes." They said, "Oh my God how long?" My mother said, "I heard everything." She told them to get their books and she took them home. My mother was gifted and didn't know because she wasn't raised in church. She was gifted by God and could sense things and dream. Things would come to life just like she dreamed they would happen. It took Bishop Cooper and Elect Lady Cooper coming to our town to start a church and lead bible studies to help my mother understand. They would have Bible studies at different people's homes. They started teaching my mother about the spiritual gifts of God, discernment and how to pray. Many times you can see things and it doesn't happen and there are times God allows you to see things so you can pray it away. Mother didn't know any of this before the Coopers came and would just say "Oh, I had a dream," and that would be it. Six of us have this gift. I was the first sibling and God started to use me and I would show them how. I watched other prophets. God is so awesome!

My mother said at the time that I was trying to tell her about the babysitters' abuse, and she didn't believe it. I would try to explain to her that they made us do things like take off our clothes and coerce Murphy to touch us in places and they made us touch Murphy too. Murphy would cry and say, "I'm going to tell my mama, I'm going to tell my daddy! You're not supposed to do this!" They would hit Murphy and slap him in the face and tell him to go sit in the corner. My mother said, "This is what my daughter was trying to tell me."

She had to deal with a lot of folk talking about my gift. Often when a child has a gift, people will first say the child exaggerates a lot, or the child likes to tell little fibs. But when Mom and Dad eventually found out I wasn't lying or just trying to get attention and believed I was telling them the truth, my mom apologized to me and hugged me. She used her wisdom and didn't tell Daddy. God saved him 11 years after she got saved, but he was known for having a bad temper. He might have come to the church and caused a big scene that could have split the church up or we would have had to leave and go to another one.

Mother used her wisdom and insight. She kept things to herself for a long time before telling Daddy. It was the late Bishop Cooper at that time and Elect Lady Cooper that said she needed to ask God to show her how to share this information. He needed to know because I was his daughter.

～ How I Was With Men ～

I really went through it emotionally. I would ask myself why I was the way I was with men. Why didn't I like for them to hold my hands, hug or touch me? I was bitter. I was angry and afraid. I was very uncomfortable around men and did not want to be left alone with my uncle ever again. My mother said for a long time I would run whenever he came around. If he was at the house I would leave the front of the house and go back to my bedroom, shut the door and hide in the closet. I had to get some-where where I felt safe. I needed to bring these things to the surface.

I became an angry person and this part doesn't make me feel good. I got angry with my grandmother and my mom. I felt that they could have protected me better. The truth is they could not. My mother couldn't stay with me that day. She had to go back home and take care of my brother and sisters. I had to come to grips with that. I'm careful how I say things because this ordeal has bothered my mom all these years, even to this day. She may not say it, but my mother felt guilty for a long time. To help ease her pain I would sing to her and make up songs to let her know that she was my hero. We would hug and she would be crying. My intention at the time was not to be evil, hurt her, or throw blame. Never! At that time, being a 12 year old up until about 20 years old, I felt something could have been done better. But God had to deal with me. Prophet Floyd Brown and his wife were two of God's special agents sent to help pull me up out of the muck and mire that I had been stuck in.

II Timothy 2:11 says Satan takes advantage of us because we're not aware of his devices, so I've learned God's secrets. If you listen to my messages you will find them to be healing. If you go back and get old tapes of my messages and even those I preach today, you'll find I'm directly involved in the healing ministry. Emotional, mental, and physical healing. It's real. God helped us. We should have been in therapy. God helped my mom until my dad got saved and then later handled other family issues.

All of the powerful men in my life were pastors and all men of God. They would have lost it if my mother had told them everything. When my daddy did finally find out years later, his eyes got very glassy. I never remembered seeing him crying and crying and crying. It was obvious when my father was very touched by something because his eyes would become very glassy. You might see one tear come out of the left corner of his eye. He said these words, "Betty Ann, I'm so glad I'm saved. Because I would have called my Army Buddies and we would have lynched somebody." Being the good mom that she is she immediately said, "No honey, we are not going to think like that because the bible says we have to be careful what we say. God is going to get them." And he would say, "I'm just telling you where I am. I'm just letting you know. This is how I'm feeling." My mom was smart and did not tell my father until my uncle had died. She is not a fool.

About six of us brothers and sisters got together after we grew up and asked each other why we thought our uncle did these horrific things. We concluded that he was probably abused himself as a boy and that may have been the reason he became an alcoholic. He could have been fighting dark memories of his past and dealing with his own demons as an abuser.

It wasn't ever confirmed, but we tried to put two and two together and felt it had to be an uncle or even a brother, somebody in the family. His family didn't attend church and were raised on a farm in the country. Their mom had that Juke Joint. It could have been someone from the Juke Joint. Someone sitting in there and watching them. We just don't know. She sold alcohol, cigarettes, and booze. People would get drunk and dance, and we saw them twisting and gyrating. Fats Domino and Sam Cooke would be playing on the juke box. If it indeed happened that our uncle was a victim of abuse, it could have happened in many ways. We do know that he was bitter and dealing with something. Doctors today say that hurt people, hurt people. His heavy drinking may have been his vehicle to forget.

∽ *The Gifted Seer* ∽

When I was five years old, I got saved in a revival service. The Holy Spirit fell, and I began to tremble and dance in the spirit. After a while, I started speaking in tongues. At the age of five, the power of God would always fall on me. See, I was dealing with the gift God gave me while I was in my mother's womb. Gifts come without repentance and many people don't understand that. Adults are not the only ones who are gifted. Children are also gifted, and don't know how to operate with their gifts. They don't understand what it is.

Why did I see a face protruding out of another man's face? Why did I see a face protruding out of the side of a lady's face or from the back of her head? Why am I seeing spirits walking around in the house or other persons' houses that we visited? No one else could see what I was seeing. What I'm saying is real and this happened when I was five years old. I would see people walking around. They would be crying, or they would say things like "help me" and it was always something sad. I would ask my mother if she could see the lady that was crying and asking for help standing right in the same room we were in. My mother would answer no and ask me where the lady was. I would walk to where I saw her and point and she would say "No Niecy, I don't see her." After a while Mother Cooper let my mother know that I wasn't making these stories up and that I was actually seeing things in detail. I could describe down to the shoes, the clothes, if they had a tooth missing, had eye problems or if their hair was messed up. Sometimes the people would be screaming in terror and asking for help. I wasn't frightened by what I was seeing either. My grandfather was gifted too, and his father started explaining what was happening to me with my dad. They called me sister and would say, "the gifts are coming alive in you. Your great-great grandmother had them too." My grandfather on my dad's side explained that my great grandmother Leda was also gifted. People thought she was crazy because they thought she was talking to herself, but she was talking to the spirits she was seeing. She would talk to them and she would pray.

At first, my parents would tell me to be quiet and stop. They would send me to the car if we were out, scold me and tell me to be quiet because I wasn't seeing anybody. I would sit there with water in my eyes while the people would reach out to me asking questions. I started hearing things and conversations. Once while everyone was asleep, I jumped up and went to the front of the house. My father followed me and asked where I was going. I told him I thought he and Mother were up there talking with somebody. Someone was having a conversation and I heard their voices. My daddy would say, "That's all right, come on." Sometimes we would fix a little snack or a sandwich with a glass of milk. We would eat together and then go back to bed.

God gives us these types of gifts so that we start praying for the people we see. I had to learn that. He's trying to show us something is going on or a neighbor is dealing with something. You'd be surprised at what your neighbors are dealing with. So the Lord started using me to help people and give them information on how to handle things. He gave me different scriptures to read that deal with warfare. I studied Ephesians 6:12 for one year. "For we wrestle not against flesh and blood, but against principalities, powers and rulers of darkness in this world."

Often we don't teach a lot of things in churches. I was thought to be a bad person. People said I was lying, that I was off and making things up. People were told not to deal with me instead of trying to help me.

Even if they thought I was wrong, why didn't they try to teach me what they thought was right?

I sincerely wanted to understand. That's why when I see gifted children now my heart drops. I go to their parents and let them know he or she isn't lying. I explain that I was once just like their children and was ridiculed, pushed aside and called everything but a child of God. After a while you run and start denying your gift, close your eyes and pray that it will go away. Eventually it subsided, but as I grew older and became ordained as an evangelist, I was accepted as a prophetess. When I traveled overseas it started to happen again but this time the Lord said, "Now you know how to handle it." He had to prepare me very early so when the time came for me to walk in it, I would not consider it strange. God in me has helped so many children. Hundreds of children who were born gifted and their parents as well.

Chapter 3

Aunt Joann's Words

There was no shortage of love in my family. We were a large brood inclusive of siblings, cousins, aunts, uncles, grandparents, and extended family.

Not one thing did we withhold from each other. If we had it to give, whatever that might be, we met the need and were happy to do so. We were proud bible-believing Christians.

But even in the best-case scenario, if there is a crack in the foundation, the devil, a most manipulative enemy, will wedge his influence into our psyche, and capitalize on our best intentions!

Aunt Joann, my mother's sister, rest her soul, was one of the sweetest and kindest people I've ever known. She and my mother were very close and for years people thought my mom and Aunt Joann were twins because they followed each other everywhere. Aunt Joann was never far away. Whenever my mother moved, Aunt Joann moved too, and she always made sure she lived across the street from us. If my mom moved to the north side, she would move to the north side, and vice versa. Whatever church my mom attended; Aunt Joann also would attend that very same church! My sisters, brother and I loved it. She had six children, my mother had ten and we all got along well. To this day her kids and all of us are very close.

My dear, sweet Aunt Joann who I wouldn't trade for anything in this world, often responded to me with pity. This was her way of showing me love. For example, in the most loving, lullaby tone she would *always* say, "Duranice, you will never be as smart as the others because you were born two months early." Or, "You will never accomplish anything great in life because you are always sickly." Every time I had to go to the hospital, for whatever reason, she would say, "Duranice, out of all Betty Ann's children, you are the only one in and out of the hospital, you've already had two operations!" Getting raped by my mother's baby brother when I was 12 years old added fuel to her innocent remark, "Everything negative that could happen always happens to you!" She'd say.

These remarks do sound harsh when reading them off this black and white page, but these statements were wrapped in tones so soothing and kind that I consciously didn't see them as weapons and chains that in actuality were wounding and kept me bound for years.

She never raised her voice or condescended me when she spoke. Whenever she shopped, she brought something back for me. If she bought outfits for her daughters she would also buy an outfit for me. She would say, "Duranice, I'm going to give you a hundred dollars for your birthday and Duranice I'm going to give you a hundred dollars for Christmas!" and she made good on her promises!

If I didn't do well on a project, didn't pass a test or if she found out people laughed and talked negatively about me, my Aunt Joann would take me out and treat me to something nice.

Speaking honestly, Aunt Joann was like my own little god. I always quoted her and not what the word of God said. In conversations with people I would give my aunt the credit, "My Aunt Joann said God understands, my Aunt Joann said God is a merciful God, my Aunt Joann said this and that. I did not give God sole credit.

Because she rewarded me all the time, everyone was blindsided. No one was worried, scared, threatened, or troubled because everything she did was done in such a loving way. She was not trying to hurt me.

All of these negative compliments were deposited into me for years and I grabbed onto all of them with a firm grip. Her words and opinions became my spiritual crutch. I leaned on what she spoke over me and was comforted, not knowing her words were forming negative beliefs about myself that I incorporated into my life. Low self-esteem and I became the best of friends.

A prophet visited my mother's church and spoke a word over her saying, "I don't know how you're going to do it Mother Pace, but Aunt Joann is going to stifle Duranice and keep her from doing her best. She has greatness in her but as long as you allow your sister to keep doing what she's doing, though she doesn't mean any harm, it's not helping. Duranice will always be looking to be rescued and for a helping hand."

Many people experience these types of relationships without realizing the great damage it causes. They have someone to lean on, a seemingly sturdy post, and don't really have to do anything them-selves because others do it for them. Sometimes we exclusively depend on other people's prayers for us. I'm not saying we don't pray at all. Five-minute prayers are okay but building a relationship with God and growing in great faith takes time. One must bathe themselves in prayer and study the Word of God to know Him in a personal way and be guided. This is a never-ending practice. God is eternal. We can never learn or know too much about him. There are so many believers who remain working in ministries or businesses that God has mantled to others too long, and don't take the time to go to God for ourselves to find out how he wants us to operate. We don't spend time with Him to seek him to find out what he wants for us, separate and apart from others. We want microwave answers to things, so we begin to trust more in human beings rather than the God who created them. This is why God gets angry with us at times. We make gods out of people and dismiss who He is. God is not an inanimate object roaming the skies. He is not a robot that dispenses blessings out of a machine when we place a minuscule coin of prayer into it and assume parents, pastors or friends' prayers will carry us through life. This is misguided thinking. When we live this way, we find our own spiritual growth is stunted. When these crutches are removed, we find we are unsteady, doubtful and fear-ridden. God spoke to me saying, "I'm the one who helped your father, I'm the one who provided for him. You need to learn how to let me be your only God."

When Aunt Joann died, the tie binding our souls began to break. I heard cracking, tearing and the sound of an old, hard mold breaking. I believe the Lord was pulling me out of that old mindset. The sounds I was hearing were the ties, cords and rope snapping that were intermingled and woven in my mind and soul's fabric.

The deep fog of fear I'd grown accustomed to began to dissipate and clear. I even began to feel a sensation of floating. The faith I had placed in others was now being placed in God. My faith meter shot from ten to one thousand. I began to study the word incessantly and desired it to live and breathe inside of me. I shared all of this with my mother and she broke out in tongues and said, "It's done."

⁓ *That's Why I Took Them* ⁓

There was a time I sported a real bad attitude and I had to repent. Yes, I'm human and I had a rotten attitude with God.

You may find this funny, but this is truly how I was. My car note was due, my rent was due, my light bill was due, and I didn't have any groceries. I just fell back on the bed and said, "If my granddaddy was here, if my grandma was here, I would have my car. I would have my rent paid. I would have my grocery bill paid." A good old fashioned temper tantrum is what I had the nerve to exhibit, and the Lord let me have that tantrum to get all of that out of my system. When I was finally done huffing and puffing, He said to me as clear as a bell, "That's why I took them." I didn't get it! So I said, "Why God?" and he answered saying, "you were dependent on them more than you were dependent on me. Didn't I say in Philippians 4:19, 'but my God shall supply all of your needs according to my riches in glory?'" I answered, "Yes Lord." The Lord replied to me, "You don't depend on me. You look to your daddy, your brother, your granddaddy, your uncle, your mother, your mother's mother and your daddy's mother, your aunts, and their husbands. You were looking to them." He said, "That's why I took them. Because you looked to them and loved them more than you love me. You depended on them more than you depend on me."

I'm telling you the absolute truth! If one of them didn't have what I needed, one of the others did. Sometimes all of them had it and each one gave me a little bit, and I ended up having a little extra. So yes, I admit, I had a bad attitude because it felt as though all of my safety nets were snatched away from me.

God began dealing with me and got my attention right in my bedroom. I finally cried out to God saying, "No Lord! I'm sorry Jesus,

I love you Jesus!" Then He led me to give him a 3 Day consecration; a fast from midnight to noon for three days straight. It wasn't hard or strenuous. I drank water and juice and was guided to study the books of Psalms and Proverbs. He had me write everything I needed to have done for me. He also had me write down what my daddy was to me, what my brother, uncle, and Grandparents were to me. When I finished writing it all out, all I could say is that they were supporters. They supported me financially and emotionally. I really didn't go to God much, only after I could not get what I needed from my family first. God said "No, what I want you to do is start coming to me first. I want you to help others." He said, "You will write the book but it's going to be my timing." He continued, "I want you to help others because there are so many like you. They won't admit it and won't openly share it. You've got to find a way to put it in your songs and your messages."

God challenged me to start doing this. My brother has been gone now for six years. This past October 11th, 2019, my daddy has been gone for eleven years. My grandparents have been gone for 30 years or so.

Some folks laugh and don't take me seriously when I tell them it was only five years ago when I had this encounter. When I preach I say things like, "I want you to know that God wants you to totally trust him. I want you to know I have been in church all my life and saved since the age of five, but God just delivered me 5 years ago, 6 years ago, 8 years ago. He delivered me from totally not leaning on him. I was dependent on my daddy, I was dependent on my brother, my uncle. God said, 'I want you to depend on me!'" After a while, folks begin to stand and lift their hands. Some cry and others hold themselves as they rock back and forth while thinking in their minds, "Oh my God, who told this lady? How did she know this?" God said he still loves us, and didn't stop because we did this, but if we want to get to know him, draw closer to him, and be used more by him, we must move to higher levels of anointing by totally depending on Him. In the book of Proverbs, he instructs us to not lean to our own understanding but in all our ways acknowledge Him and He, not granddaddy, not our uncle, not Grand-mama, not auntie, but HE shall direct our paths. When the message is over I can see that many received it. They are gracious and thank me for helping them and let me know that word was for them.

Don't let God have to take your loved ones to get your attention. Don't let God have to take your loved ones out of your life in order to make God your Lord and Master. He wants to be Lord! Oh, I can preach this thing now!

There's a song that the renowned James Moore sings called, "I Was There All The Time." I walk up to people, grab their hand, look them right in the eyes and sing the lyrics because I want them to connect personally, in their heart of hearts. I still cry and it still ministers to me.

☦

Chapter 4

Daddy Got It

My parents were prayer warriors. My mother still is! Fasting and prayer in our home was considered a normal practice. Turning our plates down, incorporating added discipline and self-control over our appetites and spending intimate time with God through prayer and study of His Word are necessary spiritual mechanisms to survive life's ills and to grow in faith.

During this one particular season, my mother chose to sustain a 21 day consecration. There were things she needed God to do for the entire family. One, she wanted my father saved once and for all, and two, Mother was believing God to heal me physically and emotionally.

My dad was at one church and Mother was at another. My daddy always loved to say, "Baptist born, Baptist bred. When I die I will be Baptist dead."

Around this time, a lady would come up to the top of the street and stand on the corner where we lived. We always had a corner lot, Daddy loved a lot of land. He also always had an acre or two. This woman would regularly come and stand right there at the corner of our yard. About 10 minutes or so after she stood there all of a sudden Daddy would say to my mother, "Betty Ann, I'll be right back, I got to go somewhere. I've got to make a run." Of course, me being gifted sensed something wasn't right. I pulled my brother and my sister Phyllis together and asked them if they had noticed anything out of the ordinary about this lady. I explained what I had been observing. "Once a week or so she comes and stands right there at the corner of our property and all of a sudden 10 minutes goes by and Daddy is heading out the door." I asked them, "Have you all ever noticed that?" Murphy said, "I sure have!" Phyllis said she noticed it too, but nobody said anything to each other. Now we were all in deep cahoots as brother and sisters. We were going to watch this to find out what was really going on.

Our mother was just as cool. I mean when I say still carrying on for us, cooking, making sure dinner is ready, making sure clothes are washed, and we didn't have a dryer so we were hanging clothes on the line and when they dried from the warm sun we would bring them in. She was being a wonderful mother. She'd gotten saved 11 years before Daddy did and so she lifted a prayer saying, "Lord I'm tired of this!" She shared this after we got older. This thing between my dad and this lady went on for a while. I went to her about two years later. I let my brother and Phyllis know that I was going to tell Mom what I knew. And I asked them to pray for me while they were at it. If I got in trouble, well, I'd just have to be in trouble. I went to Mother and told her that I had been praying, that I'd seen some things and the Lord had been dealing with me. I said, "Mother, I believe Daddy is seeing this lady that comes every Friday. She comes and stands at the corner of our street and shortly after Daddy is in his truck she takes off walking down the other side of the street. She's got her timing down pat too. So I asked my mother if our dad was seeing and messing around with this lady. That's the best way I knew how to put it. She said, "Oh my God baby, how long have you been noticing this?" I said, "Mother a long time, about two years now and I'm not the only one." Mom exclaimed,

"What?" She asked who else knew. I said, "Murphy and Phyllis. Mother, we talked about it." She said, "You all have? Oh my god listen, you can't go anywhere with this. I want you and Phyllis and Murphy to be quiet and just pray and keep loving your father. He's going through a phase right now, oh but he loves you all and he loves me and we're going to be all right. You don't have to worry about anything!" You see she assured us and made us feel safe again. She was letting us know that we didn't have to worry about anything. We weren't going to lose our daddy and he loved us. Sure enough when I say that particular year was the year... a couple of weeks before Easter Sunday she said she thought it would be nice to invite our father to church for the Easter program to see the play. "Just invite him. You have never invited your father. "Why not invite him this year?"

I had invited him before, but he does a lot of things at his church and can't really come that often, but Mom encouraged me that if we invited him, we would get a different response. I told my mother I would invite him. She asked me to let Murphy and Phyllis know. Sure enough, when he got home, we ran to the truck to get his lunch box. One gets a jacket, one gets the hat and we're each hugging one leg, so excited to see him. After a while, he washed up and got fresh for dinner. When he got to the table she had already cooked a steak and I made the gravy. He loved mom's cooking. There was homemade bread too! While he was in his happy spot eating that good food we descended upon him and excitedly asked him if he would come to see our Easter play and that we really wanted him to come see us recite our speeches. We nearly begged him! Daddy said, "Well, when is it?" and I said, "Easter Sunday, which is Sunday after next. And it's going to be at McCulloch." He said, "Well alright we will see." He continued, "Betty the children are doing an Easter play and doing speeches." She said, "Yes, they do it every year and they really want you to come this time." Daddy said, "Well, all right, we will see if we can make that happen." Sure enough, Mom stayed home from church and finished cooking Easter Sunday dinner while the rest of us cleaned up and got in the station wagon headed for Easter Service. The power of God, through our pastor the late Bishop Cooper fell in the sanctuary. He came into the audience and began to say what God had given him. Before I knew it Daddy hit the floor. His brown suit later turned grey because he was rolling on the floor. Yes! When he got up on his feet he could hardly stand, he was buckling and speaking in tongues and we were all screaming, "Thank you, Jesus! Thank you, Jesus! Daddy got saved!" His mother was one of the church mothers and she came over and just grabbed him and cried out, "Thank you, Jesus!" This all happened at approximately 4:30 -5:00 p.m. My mother told me she knew the Lord was saving him. She thought to herself, "Wait a minute we usually get out of church at 2:00 p.m., what is going on? Something's going on?" The Lord told her not to be alarmed, nothing bad had happened and there were no accidents. God told her that He saved him, and she was getting ready to see for herself! Mother had stayed home to finish cooking dinner. She always had a big Easter Sunday dinner. Mother usually cooked everything 2 or 3 days before Sunday but this time she said, "I'm going to try some-thing different. I'm going to go on and wait and make the bread on Easter Sunday and Daddy will go ahead and take everyone to church. I'm going to stay and cook and make sure everything is fresh. She did it that way on purpose because the Lord told her to. When I say she cooked a ham, chicken, turkey, all of it! All the trimmings, my mom did not play! She was a serious cook and could throw down on peach and blackberry cobbler.

With the help of God, my brother drove back to the house. Daddy told him he could do it. Murphy did and parked without getting into an accident or getting a ticket. The power of God was still on my father in the car. He was still quickening and jumping and speaking in tongues and he couldn't drive. We were all like, "Daddy got it! Daddy got it!" When he got out of the car we all grabbed him. My mother came to the door and began to scream out, "Hallelujah thank you, Jesus," because he was calling out her name, "Betty, Betty, I got it, Betty Ann, Betty I got it, I got it, I got it, Betty Ann!"

That was the result of her fast of only water and juice for 21 days. He was so happy and from that moment on we all went to church. He studied his Bible. Daddy loved to study, and we would read to him. Mom would say, "Come on and read for your daddy." Every Saturday we would study our Sunday school book together and he eventually started teaching Sunday School.

All of this happened at my mom's COGIC church. He was a member of the Baptist Church when he met my mother when she was 19. Eleven years later she joined the Pentecostal church. When Elder Cooper put up a tent in our town, for three months my mother started slipping into it and the Holy Ghost grabbed her from the back row and carried her down to the altar crying and asking God to save her. That happened at Hayfield Church of God in Christ. Then the Lord blessed us with more members, and we moved to Valley View. The first church could only hold 150 people, but Valley View held 800 people. So Daddy got saved and immediately after three months he was made a deacon! After another three or four months he started studying to be a minister.

∼ *I Loved Church With Daddy* ∼

My parents married fairly young. Mother was 19 years old and Daddy was 24 years old. He was 35 when he got saved. He had been in the Army and took a military approach in the way he handled life.

I loved to go with my Daddy to his Baptist church. I would cry. That's all I had to do was cry, "Oooh, I want to go with Daddy, I want to go with you Daddy!" He'd say, "Betty Ann, get Niecy ready, she's going with me this morning." I loved how they spoiled me at his church. They gave me a lot of attention because I was Murphy's girl. Daddy could sing with the lead singers and he was so handsome. He was the member of a mainstream quartet that travelled. My Daddy has albums, big old albums. My mom has put them up in a box. They never made it to the creation of CDs, but they got the albums with the big photographs. They did live recordings because that's how they did it for them. Blacks at the time didn't have the money to go into the studio so you found a man that knew how to do all of that from his car. It was called Sam's truck. Sam had everything that you needed in his truck to record. All he needed was three or four hours. He would come in, set up in the church and when he got through setting everything up, he was ready. Even though they were recording secular music they would use the rooms in the church and the church would make money. This church wasn't so strict. They smoked cigars after church service, lighting up their cigarettes, and you might hear a little curse word. So they didn't have a problem with people recording secular music inside their church. You just couldn't tear up anything and you had to make sure you cleaned up after you were done. I helped clean up many times. When it was all said and done, they'd give that Pastor two or three hundred dollars. Everybody was happy!

Yes, my Dad made errors, haven't we all? Without stories of poor decisions and indiscretions, we wouldn't have a testimony to help the next person as we pass along.

Chapter 5

Thyroid Cancer

In August 1974, I began suffering from symptoms of hyperthyroidism. I started to experience hair loss from my ears up, started shaking and couldn't hold my water or drink anything. I had bad headaches and my eyes grew big and protruded. I had to drink from straws because I couldn't hold a glass, my mother cried out saying, "God, you have to give us a miracle again." She said I was starting to look like an old woman. I was aging and looking old. Radioactive iodine was given to me to kill off part of the thyroid to keep it from excreting excess thyroxine. The doctors kept an eye on it, prescribed a Synthroid medication that I took once daily for a short while and things got better.

Four years later, in 1978, I had my first bout with thyroid cancer. My parents were so sensitive toward my emotional well-being. They didn't want to tell me how serious my condition was back then because they wanted to protect me. When they learned the gravity of my condition, they didn't think it was good for me to know as they thought it would really upset me, so they didn't tell me everything. The doctor would say only so much around mom and dad with me in the room, so he asked me to go sit in the lobby and they kept my mom and dad in the room and told them everything. Dad's poker face was strong. It was always hard to tell how Daddy felt because he was a military man and very disciplined, but Mom was different. I could tell when she was dealing with pain because her eyes would fill with water, become very glassy and she would constantly wipe them. Since they were acting cool, I decided to act cool too.

∿ *Supernatural Healing* ∿

It was determined that I have an operation to remove half of my thyroid. The cancer was in full force. I could not continue to take the pills because we could not afford them, but Daddy being a man of faith said, "Duranice we are going to believe in God. We can use the money somewhere else so come on Mom, Daddy's going to pray and we're going to believe in God for your complete healing." There were so many of us, Daddy said we just couldn't afford it. With Mother on one side and Daddy on the other, they prayed the prayer of faith, "Father God, you said in third John, that above all things you wanted us to prosper and be in good health even as our soul prospers. Now Father, I need you to heal our daughter because we can't afford her medication…"

Believe it or not, I finished that last bottle of medicine and Mom and Dad didn't buy one more pill! Ever since then I have been walking in divine supernatural health.

I am a miracle because there were many things that were supposed to have happened to me that didn't since the operation, a dozen things.

I have seen God through the angels, and they have visited me. God has sent angels to me in the form of an old woman, or an old man. They always come to me in the form of older people. They've said things to me that they should not know. Being a stranger they shouldn't know what they are saying to me. Immediately God says to me, "Are you hearing me?" I'll look at them and say, "yes God" and after they get through I promise you I can look away for a minute to look in my purse or to get a tissue and I look back and they are gone. The Lord has said to me many times, "I promised your father and I promised your mother, that I would heal you as long as you live for me. If you keep seeking me Duranice, I will provide for you, guide, protect and heal you. Every time you need healing, I will heal you."

I was told I would never sing again and did lose my voice. I was cracking very bad and could not sing without cracking. During six months of recuperation, I had to write everything. They told me I could not talk at all. Dad and Mother were old school and believed you should do everything the doctor said to do. But when I first started talking that's when my brother came in. I would squeak out a word maybe two. He would bring books over and we'd read bible stories. I had a perpetual serious hoarseness and made croaking sounds. Like someone who had been preaching for six weeks without a break. When I tried to sing a song it felt like the notes were stuck dead center in my throat and couldn't break free. I sounded like an old croaking frog who could barely croak himself. My brother looked at me as tears welled up in his eyes. I'd never seen my brother cry. He commanded me, "Duranice sing!" He sounded like a commander in the army. With tears in my voice and barely audible I told my brother, "I can't." He said with all his might, "Yes you can! You're gonna sing again. Don't worry about the cracking, does it hurt? C'mon." He got orange juice, honey, and spirit of peppermint. Our mom and dad were imploring him, "What are you doing to that girl?" He pleaded as he explained to them, "Duranice is going to sing again, she's gonna sing again, God told me mama, God told me, she's going to sing again." Every time I would say I can't do it, he would repeat over and over again, three or four more times, "Yes you can, yes you can, yes you can, c'mon, say what I say!" Just thinking about it right now causes me to lift my voice and praise God for bringing me through this very difficult challenge. If it wasn't for my brother's faith I don't think I would have made it. God rest his soul! About a year afterwards, when I came through, he said, "Come here Duranice, come here girl. Sing Amazing Grace." This time I started singing, at first simple and soft, "Amazing Grace how sweet the sound" then I'd clear my throat a bit and continue singing a little bit more. He was just crying and looking at me

He was with me during the whole process and had seen me from day one. He knew I couldn't do what I'd just done. So my voice went from literally nothing to being able to sing a melody. My brother says I have this sound in my throat that came from all I went through. It came from God! It took a little more than one year from the operation for me to heal.

August was holy convocation month for the state, and it was time for the choir to form again. My brother kept saying, "you're getting in the choir, you're getting in the choir!" Daddy said "okay, are you ready Duranice?" I just didn't want anyone laughing at me. Dad said, "I don't care if they laugh at you, you just keep singing" and sure enough, my voice came back. My entire range came back. I can sing alto and soprano. I sang alto for about 10 years and my range came back. God healed me.

Chapter 6

Rat Poison

In 1993 I traveled to Rochester New York to minister during a five-day revival at Faith Temple Apostolic Church. I'd been going to Rochester for about five years and was 38 years old at the time. Bishop Jerry and Lady Maggie McCollough invited me to come and preach every year. They also brought me back with a crusade team I was a member of. So many wonderful evangelists and ministers were a part of this team. Beverly Crawford, Johnathan McKnight, and others. One night over 55 gang members came to the crusade and gave their lives to Christ. I mean they put their pipes, cigarettes, marijuana, you name it, on the altar and gave their lives to God! So, the enemy was upset and determined to stop what we were doing. We were a definite threat to the Kingdom of Darkness. At the time revivals were held for a few days and nights. The evangelism teams would stay at some of the deacons, missionaries and church mothers' homes. After church service ended, Mother Williams would take us to eat at Perkins Restaurant and Bakery on Jefferson Road. I love to eat breakfast food late at night after church. My parents said it was better to eat breakfast food than to try and eat ribs and heavy food before going to sleep. About 20 of us visited Perkins Restaurant on both Monday and Tuesday nights after the 7:00 p.m. service. I've been singing in restaurants for over 20 years. When we were seated, I began to sing, and the entire restaurant got quiet. When

I finished singing, everybody in the place applauded and cheered! The people who worked in the restaurant were curious and asked who I was. We informed them I was a visiting evangelist from Atlanta, GA there to preach the revival. They were thrilled that we were there, and we began passing out flyers to the other restaurant patrons. We all were having such a great time! Both nights I ordered their delicious eggs and pancakes. We ministered at the 6:00 a.m. and noon prayer meetings, and at the 7:00 p.m. evening service. On Wednesday afternoon, while I was up preaching, I began to feel bad. I didn't know what was going on. I felt like I was losing my breath and started seeing black spots coming before me. It felt like four or five men were squeezing me in the middle. I remember looking at Johnathan McKnight who was over by the crusade team and Beverly. Something was desperately wrong with me! I looked at Beverly and said, "I'm going to need you to help me finish this out, I'm not feeling good." I left the pulpit as quickly as I could and barely made it to the restroom. Once I made it through the door I fell straight down on my knees and started calling God's name, "Jesus, Jesus, oh God I can hardly breathe," and I could hear Satan saying to me, "All your folks are in Memphis and here you are on a crusade team with these apostolic people. I'm going to kill you right now. You don't have anybody to protect you now. All of your sisters, your brother, and your mama and daddy are at the holy convocation in Memphis and can't help you."

The sound of those words were so dark and evil. I began crying out, "Oh Jesus, the blood of Jesus!" I will never forget it! Mother Smith, who has now gone on to be with the Lord, came into the restroom! She didn't ask me what was wrong because she saw me on my hands and knees making these strong gut-wrenching sounds and gasping for air. I couldn't breathe at all and wanted to vomit even though nothing would come up. Mother Smith put her hand on my back. Her timing was impeccable. One would think she could actually hear Satan hurling his horrible and diabolical threats at me. She firmly placed her hand on my back and with great authority proclaimed right there on that bathroom floor, "YOU SHALL LIVE AND NOT DIE, Satan the blood of Jesus comes against you, take your filthy hands off of her!" I remember it like it was just yesterday. She reminded me of my mother, my mother prays like that! Right then, that thing lifted up off of me. It felt like my mother had stepped into Mother Smith's body. She asked me if I could get up on my feet. I said, "I'll try, yes ma'am, I'll try mother." She said, "Come on, you can do it!" So we got up, she grabbed some paper towels and washed my face because I was sweating and really going through it. She fixed me up and made me look decent and encouraged me that I could walk out of there. She then called for one of the deacons that was close by. "Deacon Nolan Williams, come quickly, get this baby to the hospital!"

∽ *DO YOU NOT KNOW* ∽

They took me straight away to Strong's Memorial Hospital. Dr. Schwartz, the head doctor came in the room and said, "Ma'am, how did you get here?" I pointed to Deacon Smith and answered, "He brought me." The doctor exclaimed, "Wait a minute, you walked in here?" I answered, "Yes sir, I walked in here." He asked, "You haven't been spitting up?" I said, "No sir." He examined me again saying, "Okay, you aren't throwing up, you walked in here, do you have any serious pain?" I sputtered out my answers taking deep gasping breaths between each word, "I - feel - like - something - is - squeezing - me - and I - can't - breathe." Seven more doctors came into the room and stood there looking at me like I was a science experiment. Dr. Schwartz asked me, "Do you not know? Your skin is yellow, your fingernails are yellow, Ma'am your eyes… everything is yellow. This is a sign of food poisoning! There's enough poison in your body to kill you. You should have died three days ago! It's amazing that you can still talk! What you are feeling is everything in your body slowly dying!" My gallbladder went completely bad, my liver had spots on it and was breaking down, my kidneys were breaking down. Dr. Schwartz then informed me that the culprit was rat poison. I was left to assume that someone in the kitchen did not care for me and put rat poison in my food. Whoever did it knew right where I was sitting and no one but me was affected by it. The restaurant no longer exists in Rochester, NY. I have since visited the city back in March. The mayor and clergy invited me back, apologized and gave me a proclamation in front of the whole city. They said, "We're sorry about what happened to you, but we want you to know that we love you and would never try to kill you. We are so sorry some evil people got hold of you and that you experienced such a horrible incident."

I cried so hard they had to bring me a big box of Kleenex and others started crying too. It had been 25 years since that harrowing event. I'm 61 years old now and never imagined a day like this would ever come.

⌒ Chosen In The Womb ⌒

My parents said the enemy did not like the fact that I have been anointed since early childhood. They said, "God's hand has been on you, even in your mother's womb. You were chosen by God to do the work that you are doing in evangelism."

The International Church of God in Christ made me the National Evangelist to South Korea for eight years. I traveled there every month or every other month for two weeks at a time.

Because the poison distressed my body so, I had to have surgery. That's when my second bout with thyroid cancer appeared.

Daddy believed the rat poison incident caused cancer to lay dormant for several years. I started having a lot of headaches. They operated on me and removed my gallbladder; I still have the scar today, but God grew me a new one. The medical staff calls me a living miracle because everything was restored. My kidney, liver, and gallbladder. Everything had been restored. They cut out over half of my vocal cords and my parents signed papers acknowledging that not only will I not sing again, I would also never speak again. They said I may be able to speak a word or two from time to time, but I would never be able to engage in a normal conversation ever again.

Well, my daddy let them all get through with their prognosis and we went home. I tell you, my daddy is a man of faith and he said, "Duranice, that's what those doctors said, but we know another doctor and my brother, bless his heart, the one and only Bishop M.J. Pace, would come in my room at the house every day. After my hospital stay, I had to stay inside for three months. Teachers worked with my mother and my assignments were brought to the house where I'd do my homework at my bedside. This way I wouldn't get kept back.

🌷

Chapter 7

Dreams of Marriage

We were singing in the district choir and I noticed him smiling at me. One day after service, a young man named Wyatt made his way over to me and asked what my name was. I told him. He then politely asked if he could call me sometime. Now my mother was standing close by because she didn't play when it came to boys trying to talk to her daughters. Whatever she was doing took second place if she suspected a young man lingering around her girls too long. This particular day she stopped what she was doing, turned toward my direction and focused on this young man vying for my attention. My answer to Wyatt's request to call me was, "Well, I cannot answer that. You will have to ask my mother's permission." He said, "Okay, her name is Mother Pace right?" I answered, "Yes." I pointed to where she was standing, and he walked right over to greet her. She asked him how he was doing, and he told her he was fine. Then he mustered up the courage to ask if he could call me sometimes. My Mother answered, "Well, she has not finished school yet, we want her to finish high school. She has one more year." Though I know he was disappointed with my mother's answer, he respectfully responded with a humble "Yes ma'am." Do you know that he actually waited? But, he made one little mistake. He wasn't trying to be sneaky or do anything bad. He innocently wanted to buy me a birthday gift, so he asked someone for my birth date because he couldn't talk to me. He thought just maybe he could give me a special gift without causing harm. Well, he neglected to ask my mother's permission. He brought the gift to church and handed it to me. I said, "Oh my God, is this for me?" He proudly said, "Yes, Happy Birthday!" He had given me a beautiful cross necklace! Before I could open my mouth to say another word my mother had descended upon us like a hawk! "What is this?" She asked. Wyatt knew right away that he had disappointed my mom and said, "Mother I'm sorry I thought it was okay because I heard today was Duranice's birthday." Mother replied, "Yes, it is, but she cannot have it. You did not ask us. You just took it upon yourself to buy this? Oh no, no, no, she's not grown yet!" My Dad tried to intervene in my favor saying, "Betty Ann, let the boy give her a gift, it's harmless." but mom replied, "Honey, we will talk later." Wyatt apologized and mom took the necklace from my hand, placed it back in the box and handed it all back to him.

∼ *May I Call Now?* ∼

When I finished high school, he came straight to my mom and said, "Mother Pace you told me a year ago that Duranice could not have a male friend until after she graduated from high school. Well mother, if I understand it right, Duranice graduated yesterday which was Saturday," she replied, "Yes." He continued, "and today is Sunday. Mother Pace, may I start calling Duranice now?" She answered, "You are really something else. Yes, you can call her between 9:00 p.m. – 10:00 p.m. Any time after 10:00 p.m. do not call her." Then he said, "Mother there's something else, I saved the first thing I ever bought for Duranice. I saved this cross necklace. May I give it to her now as not only a belated birthday gift but as a congratulations on her graduation?" She laughed heartily, "Oh my, my! I am impressed! Yes, you can give it to her." I was so excited! So he asked my mother if he could take me out on a date and she said yes, but only if my sister Phyllis accompanied us. She said it like this, "You cannot take her out by yourself right now. She's not at that age yet and I don't think we would ever let her get to that place. It's not that we don't trust you, we don't trust the devil." We started to go out on dates and begrudgingly I really did have to take my sister Phyllis with me as a chaperone. Phyllis was the next sister under me. It still feels like it all just happened yesterday. Our first date was at Church's Chicken which was approximately 10 to 12 minutes away from my house and right next door to a park. So we bought our chicken and took it to the park. Wyatt had done his homework! At that time cars still had tape players in them. He had bought one of the Pace Sisters music cassette tapes and played it from his car while we ate. Then he told me the nicest things, "I've been watching you. I just love everything about you. You are so beautiful, you can sing and you're so friendly and you just like everybody!" By then you know I had to be smitten with him. I said, "Thank you so much!" Phyllis was sitting on a bench and eating her chicken not far away and could see and hear everything. We laugh when we reminisce about it today. Wyatt and I continued to date and went to places like the Steakhouse, bowling and skating and Phyllis continued to go right along with us. We didn't go to the movies much. Mom and Dad didn't feel it was appropriate because it was a lot like the TV, that one-eyed demon, so we had to think of other ways to entertain ourselves.

We dated like this for about one year until Wyatt approached my parents and my brother who was also our pastor, to let them all know he was interested in more than just dating me. He wanted to get married.

He went to my parents first and then to my brother and told all three of them the same thing. "I'm in love with Duranice and I really believe that she is my wife. I want to get your blessings and see what you all think about it." My parents and my brother gave us their blessings. We could continue to date but still had to take Phyllis with us. My brother was still not in favor of this because he felt we were both mature, but mother held fast to her conviction saying "That's the only way I'm going to let that happen. I still feel they don't need to be alone. Like I said, I trust God, but I don't trust the devil."

Sometimes we would go to a friend's apartment, and he would fix dinner for us there, but when it was time to propose, Wyatt had me come to his apartment alone! He had schooled my brother on everything. So, my dear brother went to our parents and told them the time had come for Wyatt to propose and to arrange for Phyllis to not come on this next particular date. Finally, Mother said okay. I wasn't afraid or scared or anything like that. I just said, "Wow! Mother's letting me go with Wyatt by myself to his apartment for dinner?" After church one Sunday, Wyatt escorted me away. Phyllis was wearing a big smile as she stood and waved bye to me. We were waving bye to each other for the first time in a long time. I thought that was so precious. She was thinking, "Wow, you mean I don't have to get in the car?" She was happy too! Happy for me, but also happy that she didn't have to go.

Our church was planted on a hill. We got in his car and as we were driving to his place, he told me he had prepared dinner for me. I told him how sweet I thought it was. We arrived at his apartment, walked up the stairs and he opened the door. Being a perfect gentleman, he asked for my coat so he could hang it up for me.

He began preparing the setting for us. Everything was so nice! He had a long beautiful red candle lit in the middle of the table in a beautiful crystal candle holder. The table was set for two with very nice china and silverware. His menu included some of the best tasting potato salad, macaroni and cheese, collard greens, cornbread muffins, a ham and a turkey, freshly squeezed lemonade and to top the whole thing off, a beautiful pound cake served on a big plate at the end of the table. Every food item had its own brilliantly colored crystal bowl. I can get hungry just thinking about it. That was one of the best dinners I'd ever eaten.

About 30 or 40 minutes after we started eating, Wyatt stood up and said, "Excuse me, I'll be right back." He walked down his long apartment hallway. He had a nice one bedroom unit that was cute, clean, and well furnished. He had excellent taste in many things. He always dressed well, with style, and drove a very nice car.

When he returned to the table I could see from the corner of my eye that he was holding a small, square white box. My heart started to jump because I knew what was getting ready to happen! He walked around my right shoulder to face me and I closed my eyes for one quick second saying to myself, "Oh my God!" When I opened my eyes, there was Wyatt down on one knee, smiling at me. I took a deep breath and with my mouth and eyes wide open thought, "Oh my God, I see this happen in movies and with my other friends, but I just never thought about it happening to me like this. Could this really be happening to me right now?"

Then the million dollar question flowed from his mouth. "Duranice will you marry me?" I exclaimed immediately with a big double, "YES, YES!" The ring was pretty and fit perfectly. I found out later that my brother was in on the entire thing. The next time I saw him I said, "So that's why you were in my face asking me all those questions about my favorite foods." Wyatt had enlisted my brother as a detective to collect all the pertinent information he needed to make our proposal night extra special. We were both very happy and very much in love.

My mother couldn't wait to hear the details and of course wanted to know if her daughter had returned home the way she left, pure. Here is how the dialogue went. "Duranice, tell me what happened!" I said, "Mother he did not force himself on me. He gave me a nice decent hug and a peck on the cheek." She said, "Are you sure?" and I replied, "Yes ma'am! Mother! That's it!" And that was the honest-to-goodness truth. I told her we took pictures and we would have the pictures for her before the week was out. He took pictures of everything! The cake, all the food, and the different China bowls and the goblets. We enjoyed a happy one-year engagement.

BUT… Two weeks prior to the wedding, I received a very interesting phone call from a man who attended one of the area's more popular Baptist churches. I choose not to divulge the names of certain people as it is not my intent to expose, hurt or disrespect anyone.

When you are called to ministry, it must be understood that to whom much is given, much is required. We have an enemy positioned and waiting to strike if you stand anywhere close to accomplishing the plan and purpose God has designed for you. Spiritually poisonous vipers are slithering around in dark spaces. We must be keenly aware at all times. Let's really go all the way back to the beginning of time when Eve chose to ignore what she already knew about God and his instructions to her and her husband. We see a snake seducing Eve's mind, her thoughts. Remember? He is persuading her to disobey God's instruction and stirred up seeds of doubt. She listened to his off-brand, wrong, and narcissistic reasoning. Of course, we all know the disaster that resulted from her lending her ear to this conniving thief. A choice she lived to regret.

Two weeks prior to our wedding, an evil influence called my mother's house looking for me. It was a young man from a popular Baptist Church in town. "Hello, is this Duranice?" I answered, "Yes." He said, "Well you don't know me, but I am acquainted with you." I responded with a slow, hesitant, "Okay..." He continued with aggravation in his tone, "We both know Wyatt, right?" I answered, "Yes! As a matter of fact he is my fiancé." "Yes, we know," he replied, and I said, "Okay, well how can I help you?" He then continued with the most puzzling statement, "We have decided to let Wyatt marry you." I said, "Excuse me?" along with another slow, hesitant and puzzled, "Okay..." Then I exclaimed, "What? You all have decided to let me marry him?" I hung up the phone.

I immediately went to my mother about it and shared what was going on. She said, "We are going to pray!"

Two weeks before we got married the serpent struck and its poison began to slowly seep into the crevices of our relationship unbeknownst to either of us. I decided to ignore the phone call altogether because I knew the enemy was afoot. He was committing the normal nuisances to try and start our marriage off on the wrong foot. I was determined not to let that happen.

⌒ *Married 1985* ⌒

When Wyatt told my brother Murphy that he wanted to marry me, Murphy shared that the Lord had begun to deal with him about putting us over the marriage ministry at our church. Murphy bought the first set of four books, literature and material that included little quizzes with yes or no answers to help us get started.

We joined in holy matrimony on December 21st, 1985, and five years later on January 13th, 1993, our beautiful baby boy DeMarcus was born.

Three beautiful years of marriage surrounded us. We had started leading the marriage ministry and it was fruitful!

We had a lot of cookouts and events. Couples would meet at our house and we'd go to different restaurants and the theater. We set up all kinds of activities for the couples to help them get to know each other and feel comfortable. My brother was concerned that a lot of people were coming to church and not getting to know each other. They would just come to church and go home because they didn't know anyone and did not speak to each other. People began to say we were different and other churches were not doing what we were doing. Nobody seemed concerned about how married couples were making it and the challenges they faced. Folks were literally surprised and confused! "You're having cookouts at your house for couples? You are all going bowling? What?" Yes, it was a strange practice at first, but everyone soon warmed up to the idea of fellowshipping together and we built a special bond that helped us all get through some challenging times.

Sometimes a tiny drop of poison can sit and wait until it is triggered.

The wife of the man that called me two weeks before I got married approached me a few months into our marriage and asked, "Have you thought anything about my husband and your husband? You know they have lunch together every day now." I said "No." She thought I was avoiding her question which was not the case. I thought the question was strange. I was like, "God what is this?" I started to feel uneasy. When feelings of uneasiness begin with me, I start to have dreams.

Toward the end of our third year of marital bliss, the dreams began. God talks to me through dreams. I would wake up in the middle of the night and my husband would see me struggling and say, "Duranice, you are soaking wet, what is it?" I would be crying out, "Jesus, Jesus!" He asked me, "What is it? Have you had another bad dream?" I would just leave it there and not answer him. I did share it with my mother, and she encouraged me to leave it be for now and not go into detail with Wyatt. She also encouraged me to fast and pray. The dreams kept happening night after night. Wyatt continued to question me about them. He wanted to know what was going on. He brought me towels to dry with and really catered to me which was so nice, and I loved that. He would bring me water to drink so I could get comfortable and warm again. I was so messed up mentally.

The dreams seemed so real. I believed they were really happening and that's why my body reacted in such a way. I saw wolves running. The dreams always had wolves that were running after my husband. They were coming at him and even entered the church building, running down the aisles. These wild wolves came through the front doors of the church. I would scream out, "Does anybody see this besides me? Is anybody seeing these wolves? The wolves are coming in the church!" In my dream the people said, "No Duranice, where are the wolves?" I said, "they're coming down the aisles, they're coming in, oh my God!" You could hear them growling, you could see their feet and they would stand by whoever he was having an affair with. That is how I knew who he was sleeping with.

I told my mother everything and she told me I needed to share all of this with my brother, the pastor. When I told him he questioned me for clarity. "Duranice, the wolves just come in and stand beside these men?" I said, "Wherever these men were sitting the wolves would go right there."

I saw their faces. God didn't hide anything from me. Three or four of the faces I saw were not at the church at the time, but one Sunday two of them walked in the door. I was sitting in the choir stand when I saw them walk in. My sister Jewel must have seen the look on my face because she asked me what was wrong. I said, "My dream is coming to pass!" She said, "Come on let's go!" I told her what just happened, and she asked me, "Is there anything good about it?" I said, "No, they're coming to destroy my marriage." She grabbed me and started pleading the blood of Jesus and prayed, "Jesus God, cover my sister now. God gives us the wisdom to fight the devil." I was able to calm down and return to the choir stand and sing. When I got home, June called to see if I was alright before I went to bed. Mother had taught us to always put things in God's hands, so I reassured her that I was fine. She encouraged me a little more letting me know that God was surely going to fix everything.

Chapter 8

He's Gay

Not only was the enemy trying to destroy my marriage, but low self-esteem reared its head again. I asked myself, "What is this?" "I keep having these dreams with these men and my husband. All these men are always bothering my husband. The doorbell rings and there are two men standing there but as soon as my husband comes to the door they turn into wolves." These men would come to socialize and hang out. They all turned into wolves. Blood dripped from their mouths like when a wild animal is eating another wild animal.

I knew the attacks were getting ready to happen. I didn't know how but I told my mother and she confirmed that yes, they were getting ready to attack. They would come in the form of friendship. She said that is why God is showing them turning into wolves. I was starting to see their teeth. They were planning and plotting how to destroy him. They didn't like that we were happy, and that God was strengthening us to be a powerful couple. They didn't want us leading the couples' ministry. They hated to hear how people were testifying about how it was benefitting their families. They couldn't stand the fact that Wyatt and I stayed together and had no plans to divorce. We didn't scream at each other but talked to one another. We had family nights with the couples at church, and now those who used to close up in their homes were all going out for burgers and ice cream! It was glorious! All of this was happening because God was using us. We were teaching the couples and they shared with us in return. The devil did not like this and sped up his diabolical plan to destroy us.

I didn't want to believe it. I wanted to believe the best for us. I decided not to ask Wyatt anything about it right away. I took the advice of my mother and prayed. I decided to try and trust my husband. I shared things with her right away. She was my counselor and not just my mom. She said just leave it alone, don't say anything to him right now. Let's continue to pray and watch them.

This man that called me two weeks before I got married started pursuing my husband. He would go to my husband's job. It all started prior to us getting married. This same man, I'll call him Warren, was also married to the woman who approached me about her husband having lunch with Wyatt every day. His wife would continue to approach me with the same type of questions, "Do you ever wonder why your husband is going to lunch with my husband? Do you know that at all? They go to lunch almost every day." I told her no, that I didn't know any of that. I told her that it was okay with me and that I trusted my husband. She responded with a snarl saying, "You are so naïve!" I said, "It seems like you know something, you want me to know what it is, but you won't tell me. Are you going to tell me?" She replied, "Well, not yet. I'll let my husband tell you." Oh, was she was a mean-spirited, bitter woman. I believe she was upset with me because I didn't allow myself to lose it when she approached me with the mess. I saw where she was going and didn't want to start anything. They thought I was pretending when I said I didn't know what they were talking about. Finally, they realized I was telling the truth, so after some time her husband confronted me and asked, "Did my wife say anything to you about me and Wyatt having lunch?" I answered, "Yes, we talked. You go to Wyatt's job and buy him lunch." He said, "Yeah and sometimes he buys my lunch." I focused on his body language and how he was addressing me. He said, "Wyatt and I are friends, you know what I'm saying?" And I said, "No, what are you trying to say?" That's when he finally got what he wanted to say off of his chest. "Wyatt and I have been seeing each other!" I responded by asking him if he and my husband were gay. He answered "Yes."

All of this happened after church on Sunday. The next day I called my brother Murphy and told him everything that happened. I told him they were trying to destroy my marriage. He told me he was going to be more watchful and prayerful.

My brother was pastor to all of us and was tired of this going on. He asked me how long I had been home with our parents, and I told him, "two or three months now." He said, "Oh no, I have got to get on this now. He said, "we are going to have a meeting." He called everybody. There were about six of us all together.

My brother had us meet in his office. He had a circle of chairs for us to sit in so we could look at each other comfortably. The man's wife sat in that meeting with a smirk on her face as if to say, "Now do you believe me?" I didn't say anything to this woman for a long time. She and one of my sisters are best friends. I was not going to let that destroy the wonderful friendship between my sister and me.

I was so glad to get away from that and grateful that God kept my mind.

I started traveling more as an evangelist, getting out and doing more revivals and had started before I got the divorce.

Four years went by then we separated for a year. After that separation, he started coming around and wanted to meet at restaurants together so I could bring our baby. DeMarcus was so young at the time.

I was so hurt I just couldn't do it anymore. I broke the news to him one night at the house. I said I couldn't love or trust him anymore. He wanted to pursue dating to get back together with me because we were still married. My thoughts would go right back to that man and his wife. All I could see was that couple and how they treated me. The deception and lies were still palpable. I was angry with Wyatt and wanted to know why he just couldn't tell me himself. I kept saying, "why didn't you tell me?" over and over again. "I waited so long because I wanted you to tell me. We are the ones in love, we were the ones that made the vows and got married."

When he finally told me he was gay I felt like I was going to die. It felt like someone stabbed me in the heart several times. I knew it was true, but I didn't want to believe it.

I tried to stay married for another four years and I couldn't do it. I apologized and never went back.

I thank God for my Godly Parents. They told me I needed to give God some time in prayer and turn over my plate. They started seeing bitterness and hatred in me. Some people found it hard to believe and said they could never see me being bitter. I was like "Oh yes I was, yes I was." I would see them and be disgusted and upset. It was my brother's church and I wanted them to just leave! My mother would say "No, no, no, no, no, I don't like what I hear." She told me you've got to give it time and prayer. I hated it. I'm so glad it was just me and my mama so I could scream out, "It's so hard!" My parents still spoke to them and didn't act nasty or ugly. That's when I said, "Okay God, is there something wrong with me?" I have the utmost respect for my parents, but I was thinking, "Hello, I'm your daughter okay? You all are supposed to be on my side! Hello? Remember me?"

The Lord told me he wanted me to share this with you and so many others. This activity stays secret in churches and marriages. It is killing people and destroying families and marriages. The Lord had me study Ephesians 6:12 for one whole year. He broke down it down for me in Hebrew, Greek, The Message Bible, King James, and Amplified versions.

"For we wrestle not against flesh and blood but against principalities and powers and rulers of darkness." He told me to tell them from this moment on, take nothing else personal. The people that transgress against you are victims of the same entity that is trying to destroy you. Look beyond the exterior at what's real. The exterior will one day blow away like grains of sand. What is on the inside is eternal.

If you have experience with homosexuality or lesbianism, I advise you to read this scripture first. From this moment on, if I'm going to be delivered and healed, if I'm going to be happy again, if I'm not going to be bitter and stop running from churches and not be a church member anymore, I must from this moment on take nothing else personal. Because it's not personal, but it is purposeful! Ephesians 6:12 runs deep through my core. Oh, I could write it backwards. He told me to tell you that you must read this first! When you read and digest this word, you will be healed; happy and whole.

∿ *I Chose Wyatt* ∿

God didn't put this on me, I walked into this. I'm the one who said, "I do," I chose him. We know what is really going on if we are honest with ourselves. I allowed a lot of things to slip before I walked down that aisle. I was warned in my spirit to not be a fool. I am the one who received that phone call.

That first tugging was God warning me. You won't find this in the Bible or in Seminary. This comes from going through trials and being disobedient. This comes from wanting to have it my way. "This is what I want, I'm going to do it at this time, I don't care what anyone says, I'm doing it!" I know that some people would cry, and others will frown when I share this. But I was taught that I must look beyond the frowns and tears when I preach. God has given me these Revelations, no one else. This message will bring powerful deliverance and not everyone is going to embrace it.

The church these men attended was known as one of the biggest churches in Atlanta. They were a higher class. Everyone was a teacher, lawyer, doctor, or nurse and made a lot of money. They were considered the upper echelon in church membership. The day came in the fourth year of our marriage when Wyatt got a call from the same man that called me two weeks before our wedding. The Lord told me to go into the kitchen, slowly pick up the telephone, and listen quietly. When I heard the voice, I knew it was him and almost started screaming.

∼ *The Venom of AIDS* ∼

The Lord instructed me to listen and this is what I heard: "What are we going to do, Wyatt? I'm sick! I just came from the hospital and the doctor said I was sick. I got it! I have AIDS, full blown! How are we going to handle this? What are you going to do about it?" I was shaking in my skin.

At this time, he had bought me an Aspen, a nice little car. I could not get out of that house fast enough. I put the phone down and Wyatt started calling my name, "Duranice, Duranice, where are you?" I told him I would be back as I was running out the door. I got to my mom and dad's house so quick. I said, "Mother come ride with me," and she said "Okay honey wait a minute, I'm coming. Let me put some things up. I was just finishing up dinner, let me tell Daddy." But my daddy said "Go on, go on and get in that car. I know when Duranice needs you. Duranice doesn't come over here like this. She has a story that she has to tell. Just turn the pots off." So, we got in the car and she asked me what was wrong. I said, "Mom you remember that call I got two weeks before my wedding, and the man who said they've decided to let me marry Wyatt? He just called Wyatt today. The Lord told me to go into the kitchen and pick up the phone real slow. Mother, when I picked up the phone, he was asking Wyatt what are we going to do about it? I'm sick and how are we going to handle this? What are we going to do, Wyatt? What are we going to do?" Mother started crying and said we had to tell my father and brother. "We have to tell them!" Then she told me that I had to get tested. When my brother and Dad learned the news they said the same exact thing. I had to get tested and right now. I went to SP Free Clinic in downtown Atlanta. I told Wyatt I had heard his conversation and that God told me to pick up the phone. He said, "I thought I heard the phone, but I told myself no one was there." I said, "Yes it was me." Wyatt said, "Duranice you've been keeping this all this time?" I told him, "I need you to know I've shared it with Mommy and Daddy and Pastor knows too. They told me I have to get tested." He said there was a clinic on West Peachtree Street, and he did not want me to go by myself. He wanted to go with me and asked, "Do you want to ride in separate cars or go together?" I told him I really didn't know what I wanted to do right then. I just didn't want to be with him right at that moment. I didn't know if I could handle what they were going to tell me. I said I would drive my car and he could take his truck. When I arrived, I was given paperwork to fill out, and waited for them to call our names. The wait was about 20 minutes but seemed like 20 years. Husbands and wives are kept in separate rooms because no one knows what might happen. All I know is when they were finished examining me, I was in the clear. "For now," they said. I asked, "Why do you say, 'for now'?" The doctor replied, "I have to say it like this, miss. If I don't I can lose my job." I asked him what he meant by that and he said "AIDS can lie dormant for 18 years in a person's body and not show one sign. It will just lay there. That's why we call it the sleeping giant because it can lie dormant in a person's body for 18 years. I'm not saying this to put fear in you. You don't have to come every year if you're not feeling anything strange." He then began to recite a list of all the things that might happen and the signs that I might look for, like finding blood in my ears, nose, or mouth. I didn't have to come every year, but he did ask that I return in five years. "We don't see any signs of it right now but promise me you will come back in five years. Even if it's not this clinic, go to a clinic to make sure you are okay." I told him okay. After ten minutes of waiting on my husband in the lobby, I heard a horrific scream and it pierced me! Wyatt was screaming, "NO, NO, NO, NO, NO!" I'm so glad there was no one else in the lobby besides me. I threw up my hands and screamed out, "Lord are you telling me what I think you are telling me?" In that moment God let me know that he had me. It wasn't going to be easy, but he had me. Whatever I decided to do he would honor. The doctor came out to the lobby and said that Wyatt could not be consoled, and they needed me to help calm him down. When I entered his room, he was bent over with his hand on his head and crying like a baby. All I could do was ask him to tell me the truth. He said, "Duranice, promise that you won't leave me." I said, "I can't do all of that. I can't handle it right now." He said, "I have AIDS, Duranice. It's full-blown." The doctor said they are amazed we've been married 4 years, and nothing had happened to me. The doctor said, "You travel, you sing, and you feel no sickness? You don't feel anything moving in your stomach, no blood coming out of your mouth, ears or rectum all of a sudden, nothing? You can sleep and you're not throwing up or anything?" I said no. The doctor was amazed and said, "Wow, where do you go to church?" I told him, "Powerhouse Deliverance Church of God in Christ, near Spelman and Morehouse." He asked when do we have service. That man came to my brother's Church to visit!

I truly had no idea Wyatt was gay. I wish I had video tapes of the services to show how nicely they all dressed. He drove nice cars and was one of the top men working for the IRS. He collected money from billionaires! He took care of me very well. Unfortunately, he is still living with all the sicknesses and has had six operations. We have remained close for our son's sake. I will never let DeMarcus forget his father's birthday. This is how God would have it. Wyatt is a family man and was there when his son graduated high school and college, and when he and his beautiful bride were married. He loves DeMarcus and DeMarcus loves him. That's where my mother's wisdom came in. The devil wanted me to act a fool.

A year later, I divorced him. I tried to hang in there but could not do it. Making love was problematic for me, as one might assume.

The dreams and everything were getting worse. Things were coming to pass almost as soon as I dreamed it. Things were happening so quickly. Going to church, praising God, hearing my brother's powerful messages, and singing in the choir, I loved that. Music was my medicine. Going to church was a strengthener but I also thank God for my parents who were spiritual guides. My father said, "Duranice, before you become bitter, nasty, and trying to get revenge; to get back at people and trying to do little things because the devil starts talking to you. Daddy's human and Mama, she's human and we know." I would just start crying and admit that yes, the devil was torturing my mind. Daddy said "I agree you've got to make the decision whether or not you are going to divorce him. You need to do what's best to save yourself and your son." He said that's what the Lord told me to tell you. When he said that, the weight of the world lifted off of me. It was like I could finally breathe the Lord's fresh air. I thought, oh God, thank you. Daddy's advice was to the point.

Wyatt and I began driving separately to church. I know people were watching because we used to come together in the same car. When I got to church, I would literally start praying right before getting out of the car, "God give me the strength to smile, help me to be nice and kind. God, please don't let me break."

My Grandmother used to say, "Don't air your dirty laundry." I prayed, "God just help me, please help me."

I wasn't happy at all and wondered if people could see that I was hurting. That's how a lot of songs came to me. A lot of my songs and messages came about because I wondered, could anybody see that I'm hurting? I would be singing, and the people would be happy. When I finished I would have to go to the restroom and splash water on my face and pray "help me Jesus", and he did. He sent prophets like Eartha Mae Brown. One day I was sitting and waiting on my sisters because we were all going to get together and go out. Fellowshipping with my sisters was my strength. My family truly gave me strength. Loving God, hearing the powerful messages and singing in the choir were a pure blessing to me. While I waited, Ms. Eartha Mae Brown snuck up on me and said, "I see you" while she's sitting down beside me. She put her hands around my shoulder and continued to minister to me. "I see you." She began speaking in tongues softly with a very dainty sweet voice and repeated, "I see you; I see you. Do not think you have gone unnoticed. God sees and he knows and he's getting ready to move for you. I see the tears and I hear the cries and God said he's going to come down and he's going to deliver you." So, there I go, with her arm around my shoulder. I started to cry with my bottom lip shaking and she said, "Come on, let it go, let it go." So softly she would speak to me and didn't cause a scene. My sisters looked around and saw me and saw Eartha Mae Brown ministering to me. That made them happy.

⁓ *I Heard God's Voice* ⁓

One morning at 6:00 a.m. I heard God's voice say, "Get up now." I always saw Wyatt off to work. After that, I called my brother and my mom and told them, "Today is the day." My mother said, "Your cousin Charles called at 8:00 this morning and asked, 'What's going on with Duranice?'" Charles lived an hour and a half away. My mother told him I needed someone to help me at that moment. I didn't want any of the furniture except for the bedroom suite and my son's and my clothes and I needed to get all of it out immediately. He said, "Give me the address and tell her I am on my way." Isn't that something? He came and got me out of there before noon yes ma'am! I left the living room and dining room furniture, the other bedroom furniture, all these beautiful things because Wyatt had bought a house full of beautiful furniture. The house I was leaving was gorgeous. I loved it, but God told me he would give me another house. The Lord reminded me what my Daddy said, "Don't lose your jolly spirit, kindness, and become mean, ugly and evil. Don't try to get revenge." When Charles got there I was ready; emotionally, mentally, and spiritually. I took a deep breath and looked around. Charles wouldn't let me touch a thing. He said, "tell her I'm on my way just box up everything!" He was a strong football player and moved that bedroom suite on his truck so quickly. I just said thank you God, locked the door, walked down the steps and got in the truck. He took me over to my parent's house and all my sisters helped move me in. Everything just worked out. God is so awesome. From A to Z he set it up. He gave me a sign to give me peace and let me know I was in his will.

Wyatt was not happy when he discovered I moved out. He called my mom and asked had anyone seen me. "Where is Duranice?" My mom put my dad on the phone and told Wyatt to calm down and let him know I was there. He said "Do you really want me to go there on the phone or do you want to come over? I think it would be best if you come over so we can all talk together." Daddy was a powerful father. He sent everyone to get something to eat and asked them to call when they were finished. Wyatt came over and my father told him I tried to stay but felt like I was losing myself and didn't want to become bitter or vengeful. He told him I wasn't sleeping or eating, and this wasn't good. DeMarcus was beginning to pick up on things and was crying a lot more. Thank God for my parents and the older Saints in the church who let me know that my child was sensing my feelings. My son would be in the baby bed, but I was in the other room crying out to God. Pleading with God how was I going to get through this. All the while, Marcus was also crying in the other room. My mom said God connects you with your baby. That first three months when a mother is carrying a child, both of them are being connected to one another. Wyatt tried and tried to convince my father, but he told him very sternly, "Yes, we do the right thing but let's do the God thing right here. You are guilty, right? You had an affair with a young man, did you not?" Wyatt said yes sir. "Duranice told us everything. My daughter is just as human as you are. She's a proud woman of God. Do you think she can just take this lightly?" Wyatt said no and my daddy replied, "I don't preach divorce, but she needs to exit this marriage before she loses herself." He said, "Nobody's tried to hurt you. You made those decisions; you made those choices. I'm not going to let you do this to her. Now she's going to be there if you want to see your son. You can even come over and eat Sunday dinner with us. We're not kicking you out. We're not going to mistreat you. Just let Duranice do what she has to do." All Wyatt could do was sit there with his hands on his knees and say, "you're right." He started crying and saying, "I'm sorry, I'm sorry, I don't know why I did it. Out of all the people in the world, why did I do this to Duranice?" My daddy said the enemy comes to kill, steal, and destroy. Wyatt was also a preacher. He's still preaching to this day, and he can preach the hair off of your head, yes ma'am! He's the assistant pastor at his church now and they love him there. His church is tolerant of homosexuality. I don't say anything. My son visited and I've been invited to preach for a women's conference. I accepted their invitation and stuck strictly to their scripture reference and theme. This gave my son time to see and fellowship with his father. I know God was using my daddy. God strengthened me to the point that we started having family nights together. We met at a restaurant every Monday or every other Monday just for my son. The Lord showed me that Wyatt was one of the world's greatest fathers because he loves and supports his son. He took care of him and paid for his education. My son didn't have to go to public school. I have to tell people that Wyatt is an excellent man and awesome father.

Moving out of that house was freedom for me. The burden I carried for so long was finally lifted.

I lived there at my parents' house for six months and then God blessed me with a house! I'll never forget it. The Lord blessed us with our own house!

My ex-husband still struggles. He is such a wonderful person and I love him in Christ. He has helped me financially and in so many other good ways. My mother saw his generosity and the way he showed how much he cared for me and our son. She believes he truly loved me. I also believe the love he had for me was real.

Chapter 9

Three Years to Live

On March 28, 2008, doctors at Kaiser Permanente had given me three years to live. At 50 years old the thyroid cancer that had afflicted me in 1978 had returned a second time.

I asked the doctors what was going on. I was starting to feel different. I was bleeding and spitting up blood. My nose would start bleeding out of the blue and my hair came out of my head in handfuls when I brushed it. I went completely bald.

Kaiser wanted me to do full chemo and dialysis, but my daddy had been on dialysis for six years, three times a week. Before he died on Oct 28th, he brought us all together and looked up at us from his bed. He told us that he didn't want us to die as he was dying. He wanted us to change our appetites and eating habits.

When the doctors tried to prescribe chemo for me, I said no sir! I'm not doing dialysis or chemo, and I'm not taking any medications. I saw how my father dreaded doing it. The medical staff was baffled at my choice and thought I was trying to be Super-Woman. I told them I was going to believe in God.

My mother had cancer and God healed her. Shaun has had cancer and He healed her too. My family has been through it but by God's grace we have lived to proclaim that He is a miracle worker. Every March 28th I celebrate God healing me and giving me another chance.

Chapter 10

Healing Begins

I n the beginning, I ran from my gift of healing.

As I got older, fear hit me when I really saw the impact it made on people. I learned you can only go so far as a preacher without studying and spending adequate time on your knees. You can't stand in front of people and say that God said what He didn't really say.

I started thinking about my life as a spiritually gifted child at 5, 6, and 7 years old. There was an excitement surrounding my gifts and older people were in awe when I prophesied. They would say with astonishment that the hand of God was on me and I loved hearing that sound. But when I got older and out of high school, in my late teens and early twenties, things took a 180 degree turn. The "wow" factor left, and people began to question if God was really the one speaking or if I was making things up. They began complaining, so I started studying even more. The older, more mature, and experienced prophets and prophetesses were well-versed in scripture. They had more wisdom because they had been practicing longer than I had. Sometimes even when God is in it, He will allow things to go topsy-turvy to show you that you aren't prepared. The sacrifice is great, and you have to be willing to lose everything you have because God wants a total "Yes."

When I was a child, people liked when I spoke and would comment, "Oh, that's so cute." They would stop and ask everyone to be silent so they could listen to what I was going to say. "The Lord is speaking to Duranice, let's be quiet... Oh my God, how did she know that?" They turn on you when you get older though and make faces as if you aren't really sold out to God. My Daddy told me to close my eyes and apologize for making them upset and that they were taking it personal. He said to tell them that I was sharing what God told me to say and that I was not taking it back because I would get in trouble. God would have to show them.

A lot of them did like what I told them because the Lord uncovered marital infidelities and affairs. He also exposed some who were smoking and drinking.

My parents taught me to go to their ear to share what the Lord would give me, but they would clown and act up. To avoid some of that behavior I would ask the Saints to start praising and worshipping God. That also helped with giving people privacy because it's not fair for everyone to hear what is private and personal. I would walk right to their ear, put the mic down and say, "the Lord said you are still smoking, drinking, and cursing. The Lord said if you can get rid of that lying spirit, he is going to heal your marriage." People would come to church smelling good with their cologne and perfume and put Listerine or chewing gum on their breath and wear the right color of lipstick. They thought they were hiding things. For the most part, they received you because you're an evangelist or a missionary. You are blessing people but can also see what they are doing behind closed doors. So the Lord would literally call their exact situation to light and they would sputter saying things like "Oh, she's a bit much for me," and others would break and cry. Some would affirm what I said, and a few admitted to the truth. Some would humble themselves and start crying and saying, "You are right, you are right, oh my God you are right! I want to get closer to God, I want God to save my family, I want God to heal my marriage." Then others simply blew me off, saying, "I know she is not talking to me," or "No, I don't receive that."

It was sad when they died. The Lord would always allow judgement to fall on them and they would die. At funerals, pastors would reveal that saints were dying from cirrhosis of the liver because they were drinking or chain-smoking. When the Lord was using me as a teenager and young adult they thought I was coming from left field. Family and friends would attend the funerals and the next Sunday would come to my parents and say the Lord was speaking through me and I was on it or they remembered the prophecy.

When I travel overseas to places like Italy, Japan, Korea, and Australia I get red carpet treatment. I love going overseas because there is no fight trying to prove anything. There are no self-righteous spirits. It's more like, "thank you, Jesus, oh my God you're right, I know the Lord sent you here." They do what God says and you see their life, and their whole family's lives change for the better. They reward you and bless you financially because many are military. A lot of them are not paying their tithes anywhere so they will give their tithe to whoever is ministering. They say they've been saving their tithes for six months or I've been saving my tithe for a year and didn't know who to pay my tithe to.

I started to shun the gift. When I was invited to minister, people started asking if I was going to speak and I would say no. I would whisper and say, "Now you know you always ask me but there are so many other young preachers and teachers and missionaries, why don't you ask some of them?" My daddy would say, "I'm going to let it go this time. They know who the Lord is telling them to invite as a speaker and they have to obey God. God may have told them to ask you. Who are you to suggest somebody else? What is wrong with you? You said God called you, now what? Did God change his mind? God doesn't change his mind." He said, "That's your flesh. Something is going on, when you get ready to tell me you tell me, because this is not the will of God." Sometimes I would just break and start crying, "Daddy it's harder than I thought it was." He said, "No it's not harder than you thought. You are getting older and your flesh wants to do something else. You want to start dating and experiencing certain things but there are things you are not going to be able to do." I was sitting there with big tears in my eyes, and I knew he was telling me the truth. He said some things you are not going to be able to do and there are some things you are not going to be able to wear. He went there and he was on it. I thank God for this day and my mother told me that God has his hands on me. King David had so much favor and he had Uriah killed after he impregnated his wife. Fortunately, he quickly repented. I apologized to my dad, but he said, "No don't tell me. Tell the Lord." He reminded me of the scripture that says to whom much is given much is required. Daddy was the first one to explain that scripture to me. He said, "God has need of you; not that he needs you, but he wants you and has chosen you to do this work at this time. You can reach folks that I will never reach." He never whipped me with a belt, but he whooped me with God's word. When he got through I was apologizing to the Lord and crying out before Him. I humbled myself, got on my knees and told Him how sorry I was. It wasn't a long run of me wanting to go where I wanted and have a boyfriend. This is just how it was in my days growing up in ministry. I wanted to wear pants. If you had a call on your life you couldn't wear pants, earrings, or makeup in my household. I was 18 or 19 years old and I didn't like that my sisters were wearing pants and makeup. They wore earrings too, so why couldn't I? Little things like that caused a big problem because I wanted to experience those things. Little did I know that my sister told me 30-40 years later that they wanted to be like me and for God to use them like He was using me. And I told them, "But I wanted to wear the earrings and pants and go out!" They told me that everybody wanted to take them out to eat, skating and bowling but nobody would ask me if I wanted to go too. My sister said, "Oh and I paid for it, you see your nephew over there? And I've never been married. Daddy was telling you and it seemed like he was strict and hard on you. We saw God and knew he had called you and we knew the power of God was on you." My sister said folks got upset because God was so on it. They thought their mess was hidden and God uncovered it and let the truth be told. She said God never missed in me and that everything I said God said, happened. If you said they were smoking it was uncovered, if you said they were drinking it was uncovered not by you, but God revealed it.

My sisters do operate in the supernatural gifts too but all of them will say that my gift is in another place.

The first time I saw a miracle was in Lakewood, Georgia on the Lakewood Fairgrounds under the tent of the late A.A. Allen and the Allen Revival Crusade team. I had to have been somewhere between 13 and 16 years old. He had a tent that held about 1,000 people. There were people of all races there. Black, White, and Mexican.

There was a movie that Steve Martin was in. My sister Shaun also sang a very popular song in that film called, "Are You Ready for a Miracle." That tent on the fairgrounds was just like the one I saw in that movie. It had a big old ramp in the front where they actually wheeled patients from greater Memorial Hospital. There was an ambulance from that hospital that pulled up to the tent and emptied people out of it onto a cart and rolled them up the entire ramp. This ramp was connected to the stage. A man named Anointed Hands would tell the patients to sit upright. Some could sit up and others could not. If they could not, he would have them raise the bed up in a chair position. Then he'd cry out "In the name of Jesus, I command you to rise and walk!" Those who were on the beds that came out of the ambulance would pull their covers off, stand up on their feet and walk across the ramp. When they arrived at the end of the ramp some of them would run and cry out, "Thank you Jesus, thank you Jesus!" One man was deaf, and the crusade team had him come up front. The man didn't move or do anything then the evangelist said, "I command the deaf spirits to leave this man now!" He would stand a step or two away from the man and say, "say Jesus," the man said Jesus! The family that brought him were running all over the place. This one boy was in a wheelchair and had one leg that was shorter than the other. His people didn't like for him to do a lot of walking. He wore one of those shoes with the big heel on the shorter leg. The minister had him take off the shoe and hold both legs up where everyone could see. Then he said, "I command the left leg to grow even with the right leg now in the name of Jesus!" While he was saying it, the leg was growing, and people would scream. You could see the leg actually moving and when it caught up with the leg that was longer it stopped. I saw it with my own eyes.

∽ My Healing Ministry Began ∽

I was about 28 years old when the Lord first used me in healing ministry. I remember grabbing this lady who was in line. She said, "I'm so sick, I just don't feel good. I'm hurting, I just want you to pray for me."

I said, "Yes ma'am, first of all do you believe God can heal anything? Do you believe God is a miracle worker?" She said yes and I said, "Do you believe God is going to heal you?" "Yes!" she answered. "I'm going to anoint you and pray for you." When I tell you that lady jumped up out of that chair, she jumped up out of that chair and started running all over the building screaming "It's gone, it's gone! I don't know what happened, but it's gone oh my God oh my God." Everybody started praising God, clapping their hands.

My daddy had the gift of healing when he started pastoring. When it was time for him to start laying hands on people oil would start flowing from his hands. We saw it and touched it. When it began flowing, he knew it was time to call for the sick. People with tumors, migraines, and headaches. When my daddy prayed, God healed the people. Many who were healed came to our church and became members.

I started watching and observing ministers who operated in the gift of healing and I loved it. My mother would sneak us out early from church and school on the weekends and Fridays. She would come to school at noon and sign whatever paperwork she needed to so that we could leave with her. They said, "We'll see you on Monday." My mother would take us to get us a Happy Meal and head straight to the tent revival. She'd say, "Alright we're going in!" The only thing we couldn't do is share this news with anyone whatsoever because a lot of people didn't approve. Many Church of God in Christ Pastors did not care for him. They would announce it from the pulpit and forbid us to go. They'd say things like, "Don't go over there to that big old tent! Don't go to the fairground! Everybody's spirit ain't right! You'll go over there and when you come back you won't ever be the same again!" Some of these ministers and parishioners operated out of fear. We saw miracles happen! We saw blinded eyes opened and deaf people come to hear again. There were people that could only lay down that left the tent walking. God used the late A.A. Allen.

∽ *I Just Want God To Use Me* ∽

When I saw it, I began to plead with God saying, "God, I want to do that. God, I want you to use me like that." My mother said, "Do you know what you're asking for? Because to be used like that you have to spend a lot of time with God. I'm not saying you can't do it, you can absolutely do it, I just want you to know." I said, "Mother, I just want God to use me." Through tears I'd say, "I want God to use me like how he uses the man in the service. I want God to use me like that too." She said, "Well you can't be fearful." I had to get rid of certain fears when it came to dealing with people with big tumors on their necks and large outgrowths on their faces. I didn't like that and at first, I was like, "Oh God NO!" My mom immediately corrected me saying, "No, you've got to hurry up right now and ask the Lord to melt, mold and shape you because you are going to see everything on the evangelistic field, but you can't be afraid. Sometimes you don't touch people, you just speak the word and let God touch them. I had to learn that.

Chapter 11

Losing the Poison

Isn't it really something when people keep you stuck in the past? There can be awesome things happening in your life but for some reason, they want to keep you locked in your past. Yes, that happened to me

Church people knew my parents and grandparents and the struggle we had with obesity. My Dad and grandmother didn't have any discipline when it came to food. If you did well in school our reward was "let's go eat!" If you sang your song well it was, "let's go and eat!" If you did great in class, you've got it, "let's go eat." Even if we did our chores or cooked a really good meal we got to go to the candy store that was out of this world. They had fresh chocolate stars and pecan clusters. I'd go in that store and ask for a pound, then three pounds and well, I just had them go on and give me five pounds of candy sometimes. Daddy and Grandma would always ask us what we wanted and without fail, I'd ask for a pound of chocolate Stars. I gained up to 485 lbs. A few of my sisters and brother were very heavy. We found out about New Life by David Gause out of Fayetteville, North Carolina. He came to Atlanta one Saturday. Murphy heard about it and went to check it out by himself. When he returned, he told us all about it and introduced us to CKLS colon cleansers that clean your liver and gallbladder. He also told us about the benefits of eating raw vegetables. The cleansers consisted of

100% cold pressed oil with lemon juice and putting it in a blender with five CKLS pills for the first 5 days of a 14-day cleanse. I'm here to tell you that the weight began to melt from our bodies.

But instead of encouraging and congratulating us, people would tell us to our faces insensitive things like, "You are always going to be big." Or "You're going to always deal with fat." I didn't understand why they said those things and asked them why they did. I would tell them it wasn't nice to say.

My brother lost 100 pounds, Shaun lost 200 pounds, my other sister Phyllis and I lost 200 pounds. I mean everybody was losing their weight. We remembered how daddy told us that he didn't want us to die the way he did, having to do dialysis three times a week. He did that same routine for 6 years. Daddy told Murphy to get us into New Life Herbal pills. But negative people will see you looking good and want you to remain unhealthy. Misery loves company, as the saying goes. Some would even say, "We've been fat partners for years, you can't leave us now." We pigged out for years together at all of the all-you-can-eat places… We stopped eating at the all-you-can-eat places. People talked negative and reminded us that our family has always been big. I believe they wanted me to put the weight back on and were really planning for me to put it back on. These were tongue-talking and dancin' church folk! The irony is that people in the world were encouraging me and telling me I could do it, but the church folk gave me a lot of negative energy.

I had to look past the insecurities of others. Remember, earlier I said, "don't take things personal." Look past the person and direct your attention to the influence behind the words they are speaking. Then tackle that with the Word of God. I know how difficult it is to overcome such extreme obstacles in life. I've had to endure many. There are so many interruptions and obstructions littering our paths. We don't need to add personal problems that don't even belong to us. We should encourage ourselves and find like-minded people who take us to new levels. On the other side of the same coin, there's an old saying, "new levels, new devils." Ain't that the truth my sistas and brothas!

My mother's face and voice comes into frame right now. She would tell me to pray and not just for myself, but for the ones who are insensitive and insecure. We have to love our enemies. This how true agape love is exhibited. "This is my commandment, that you love one another, that your joy may be full." Lord help us to achieve such heights.

Chapter 12

Created for His Good Pleasure

My life was riddled with poisonous experiences that could have taken me out at an early age. A target was placed on my life and poisonous darts were aimed with the intention to kill and eradicate my God given purpose.

One dart was crafted sharp enough to pierce my flesh and take my life before I was born. Another dart was pointed at my self-esteem and primed to keep me bound in fear and an "I'm not good enough" mind-set. Other ammunitions were gathered and prepped to break my heart into pieces from lies and deceit.

There were times that I didn't think I could make it. My heart was a monstrous weight and I didn't think I could stand. The enemy worked hard to dilute my total trust in God and make me give up. But that's okay. It did not injure me! It made me stronger and it made me lean into Christ that much more. I am a prime example, that as deadly as poison is, it cannot override God's plan and purpose for our lives.

God protected His purpose for my life. He took it and nestled it under his armor of love and protection. Though times appeared hopeless and without resolve, God showed me that miracles are real and remain available to us today.

I am supremely blessed with parents who know and trust in God as a provider and a miracle worker. My brother and sisters remain a strong support system that gives me strength in my most challenging times.

God's messengers were sent to inspire me and let me know that God saw and still sees the portrait of my life as scenic, beautiful and useful to his work here on earth.

Brethren, I beseech you, be as I am; for I am as you are: You have not injured me at all.

God turned every single one of my challenges into opportunities for ministry. The weapons the enemy tried to use against me, God ripped from his hands and directed them against the Kingdom of Darkness.

If God did it for me, I can guarantee you, He can and will do it for you too.

Duranice Pace Ministries began on December 3rd, 2008, at the one and only gymnasium in Roanoke Virginia. I started ministering over the radio every Sunday at 3:00 p.m., three days a week. It was the only gospel radio station in the city. I did that for three months until the Lord blessed me with an unexpected surprise.

One day the Lord told me to get up from my bed and go out to eat breakfast. I decided to go to the Microtel Hotel. While I was sitting there the Lord instructed me to face the buffet tables. When the owner of the hotel came into the restaurant the Lord pointed him out to me and told me to minister to him. I walked up to him and said, "Sir, how are you doing today?" He said, "Good." I said, "I'm Pastor Duranice Pace, sent all the way from Atlanta, GA to start a ministry. When I first saw you walk in, I heard the song, 'One Day at a Time Sweet Jesus.'" As soon as he heard the name of that song his face turned beet red and he began to cry. The Lord led me to tell him that God was going to heal his body.

I told him something was going on with his kidneys and he gasped. I also told him there was a sore on his wife's leg that seemed incurable, but God was going to dry it up and heal it. He grabbed my shoulders and said, "You remind me of my Grandmama. My Grandmama was an Assembly of God pastor and preached at several churches. Whatever I can do for you let me know." The Lord gave me favor with this gentleman. He offered me the second-floor conference room to hold services in. Every Wednesday evening at 7:00 p.m. I taught bible study, and on Sundays at 3:00 p.m. I held a Sunday service.

In addition to the blessing of allowing me to operate my ministry at the Microtel, this generous man let me and my son live there for $18 per night. DeMarcus and I lived there for three years.

He visited with me one day and shared that a new Extended Stay facility would be opening in Christianburg, VA in a few short months. He wanted to know if I would be interested in staying there. I'd have my own living room, kitchen, a bedroom, and bathroom. It was also the perfect location as it was near the school DeMarcus attended at the time, Christiansburg High School. Sure enough, when they completed building the hotel, the owner asked if I was ready to move and I said, "Yes sir!" I lived at the Extended Stay in Christiansburg, VA and continued my ministry at the Microtel for five years before relocating back home to Atlanta, GA after my father passed away.

I share all of this with you to encourage you to not give up on what the Lord has shown you. You have visions and dreams. You have gifts and talents that God desires to express through you and you alone. No matter how broken and defeated you might feel, there is joy waiting to embrace you. No matter how hard you've been hated on, deceived, and lied to, you have a divine judge ready to defend your cause. You were divinely manufactured and created to do great things with a never-ending warranty!

You may not look like your Purpose right now because of Poisons in your life. But Poison doesn't define you, Purpose Does.

But as for you, you meant evil against me, but God meant it for good in order to bring it about as it is this day, to save many people alive.

For Speaking Engagements, Book Signings,
Appearances, and Interviews...

Contact

LYDIA PACE
MANAGEMENT & BOOKING

Duranice Pace Ministries
5686 Fulton Industrial Blvd. SW
P.O. Box 366501
Atlanta, GA 30331

📞 678.740.1705
✉ duranicep@gmail.com
📷 #therealduranicepace

Made in the USA
Columbia, SC
28 January 2020